The Next Rodeo

D1053412

Other Books by William Kittredge

FICTION

The Willow Field
The Best Short Stories of William Kittredge
Phantom Silver, with Dirk Lee
We Are Not in This Together
The Van Gogh Field and Other Stories

NONFICTION

America's 100th Meridian: A Plains Journey,
with photographer Monte Hartman
Southwestern Homelands
Owning It All
The Nature of Generosity
Taking Care: Thoughts on Storytelling and Belief
Who Owns the West?
Hole in the Sky: A Memoir
Lost Cowboys (But Not Forgotten)
Balancing Water: Restoring the Klamath Basin,
with photographers Tupper Ansel Blake and
Madeleine Graham Blake

EDITOR

The Best of Montana's Short Fiction, with Allen Morris Jones
The Last Best Place: A Montana Anthology,
with Annick Smith
The Portable Western Reader
Montana Spaces: Essays in Celebration of Montana

The Next Rodeo

NEW AND SELECTED ESSAYS

William Kittredge

Graywolf Press

SAINT PAUL, MINNESOTA

Copyright © 2007 by William Kittredge

Publication of this volume is made possible in part by a grant provided by the Minnesota State Arts Board, through an appropriation by the Minnesota State Legislature; a grant from the Wells Fargo Foundation Minnesota; and a grant from the National Endowment for the Arts, which believes that a great nation deserves great art. Significant support has also been provided by the Bush Foundation; Target; the McKnight Foundation; and other generous contributions from foundations, corporations, and individuals. To these organizations and individuals we offer our heartfelt thanks.

Published by Graywolf Press
2402 University Avenue, Suite 203
Saint Paul, Minnesota 55114
All rights reserved.

www.graywolfpress.org

Published in the United States of America

ISBN 978-1-55597-479-4

2 4 6 8 9 7 5 3 1
First Graywolf Printing, 2007

Library of Congress Control Number: 2007924770

Cover design and art: Christa Schoenbrodt, Studio Haus

Acknowledgments

Grateful thanks to the editors of the publications listed below for first publishing the following essays:

Home: *Owning It All* (Graywolf Press, 1987), *Best American Essays 1988*

Buckaroos: An earlier version appeared in *Owning It All* (Graywolf Press, 1987). This updated version incorporates another essay, "Running Horses," which first appeared in *Cowboys and Images: The Watercolors of William Matthews* (Chronicle Books, 1994)

Owning It All: *Pacific Northwest Magazine, Owning It All* (Graywolf Press, 1987)

Who Owns the West: *Harper's, Best American Essays 1989, Modern American Memoirs, Who Owns the West* (Mercury House, 1995)

Leaving the Ranch: A slightly different version appeared in *Hole in the Sky* (Knopf, 1992; Vintage, 1993)

Reimagining Warner: *Audubon, The Literary West: An Anthology of Western American Literature* (Oxford University Press, 1999)

Redneck Secrets: *Owning It All* (Graywolf Press, 1987)

Drinking and Driving: *Owning It All* (Graywolf Press, 1987)

How to Love This World: *Big Sky Country* (Rizzoli, 1996)

White People in Paradise: *Esquire, Who Owns the West* (Mercury House, 1995)

Lost Cowboys: *Antaeus, Lost Cowboys (But Not Forgotten)* (Whitney Museum of American Art, 1992)

Bulletproof: *Ploughshares*

Contents

The Next Rodeo

Introduction

M Y FATHER WANTED to be an honest country lawyer and politician. He ended up a rancher with influential friends. When I was thinking of going seriously into writing, he said, "I've done things I hated all my life. I wouldn't recommend that." I took that as permission to court foolishness, bless him, and to get lost in work I've loved.

My mother Josephine was a single child in a blue-collar family. Her father was a blacksmith. While Josephine loved "arts"—she played the piano and sang light opera in local shows—she married into a ranch family that was rising into the ruling class in southeastern Oregon and came to believe that Dwight Eisenhower was the cat's meow. "He'll take care of people like us," she would say.

I argued with her, not my father, who was too formidable. In 1951, when I was at Oregon State College, majoring in agriculture, the topic, about which my mother and I held passionate opinions but knew little, was fairness—class relationships in America. I'd finished a college literature class where we read *Walden* and Emerson and Whitman. Their emphasis on what I took to be the native nobility of ordinary people was the gold standard for me, while Eisenhower represented the forces of power and wealth, military men and bankers—repression.

By taking his side, my mother, to my mind, was betraying

her upbringing, advocating fascism. After I called her "Missus Hitler," she whacked me across the head and wept while I sulked.

Even before college, as a boy on our ranch, I'd learned to resent the workings of power. I was sent out with the field hands in order that I might "learn to work." What I learned was to revere those sometimes bitter but often humorous men.

After I read Hemingway and decided to write, at the age of twenty-one, not long after my arguments with my mother, the working men and women I'd known and the damages they suffered were the highly emotional source of my thoughts about injustice. What else did I know?

It's a habit of mind I've never gotten over. It remained true at the age of thirty-three, when I went back to writing and was thinking of leaving the ranch, and it still is—not so much by choice but because it was the synaptic groove my mind had begun deepening.

Through the late 1960s and most of the 1970s I wrote dozens of stories about rural people, getting one or two published each year. By the fall of 1978, at the age of forty-six, I was low on momentum and finding that what I wanted to write about often involved politics and arguments that couldn't be worked into fiction without becoming didactic.

At the same time, to my good fortune, Terry McDonell started *Rocky Mountain Magazine.* He asked me to write an essay for his first issue. I said I didn't know how. He said, "I'll tell you." And he did, on the telephone—it took him maybe three minutes and went this way: (1) a set-up anecdote that introduces readers to the problem, (2) false solutions, (3) recognition of a real solution, and (4) some hint at the consequences of acting out that solution. That seemed workable, and the piece paid wonderfully by my standards, so I gave it a shot.

My first essay, "Redneck Secrets," was printed, and my deal with the world was transformed. People called and chewed me out on the telephone. I got letters (and one telegraph!). Maybe I could find an audience.

The national press was interested in almost anything about the American West through the 1980s and into the 1990s. I went to the ranchlands of northern Nevada and wrote "Owyhee Buckaroo" for *Rocky Mountain Magazine* and learned to think about environmental preservation and restoration while following Doug Peacock as he followed the grizzly bears around the highlands in Glacier Park. I found I was deeply drawn to preserving the world. I focused on family and wrote "Home" and "Owning It All" for Graywolf Press and shared a National Magazine Award for Essays and Criticism at *Harper's* for "Who Owns the West," a story about working men that then formed a chapter in *Hole in the Sky*.

Projects loomed, and loom. An ill-educated boy, I once thought no one would ever give me much that would prove very useful in terms of realizing my evolving dreams. Turns out it's been gifts all the way.

WILLIAM KITTREDGE
MARCH 2007

Home

IN THE LONG-AGO LAND of my childhood we clearly understood the high desert country of southeastern Oregon as the actual world. The rest of creation was distant as news on the radio.

In 1945, the summer I turned thirteen, my grandfather sentenced his chuck-wagon cow outfit to a month of haying on the IXL, a little ranch he had leased from the Sheldon Antelope Refuge in Nevada. Along in August we came in to lunch one noontime and found the cook, a woman named Hannah, flabbergasted by news that some bomb had just blown up a whole city in Japan. Everybody figured she had been into the vanilla extract, a frailty of cooks in those days. As we know, it was no joke. Nagasaki and then VJ Day. We all listened to that radio. Great changes and possibilities floated and cut in the air. But such far-off strange events remained the concern of people who lived in cities. We might get drunk and celebrate, but we knew such news really had nothing to do with us. Not in the far outback of southeastern Oregon.

When I came home from the Air Force in 1958, I found our backland country rich with television from the Great World. But that old attitude from my childhood, the notion that my people live in a separate kingdom where they own it all, secure from the world, is still powerful and troublesome.

When people ask where I'm from I still say southeastern Oregon, expecting them to understand my obvious pride.

༄

Jack Ray was one of the heroes of my boyhood. A slope-shouldered balding little man, Jack dominated the late roughhouse craziness at our mid-July country dances. The Harvest Moon Ball.

"He can hit like a mule kicking," my father used to say after those dances, winking at us kids and grinning at my mother's back while she served up a very late Sunday breakfast of steak and fried mush and biscuits and thick sausage gravy.

At that time I was maybe five or six years old, and I would have been asleep in the backseat of our car for a couple of hours when the shouting and fighting started around midnight. So I recall those scenes with a newly awakened child's kind of strobe-light clarity, a flash here and there, all illuminated in the headlights of 1930s automobiles. The ranch women would be crowded outside onto the porch where they could see, some wife weeping, the men out closer to the battle in the parking lot, passing bottles.

But what I see mainly is Jack Ray getting up off the ground, wiping a little trickle of blood from the corner of his mouth, glancing down at the smear on his hand, his eyes gone hard while some sweating farm boy moved at him again; and torn shirts, the little puffs of dust their feet kicked there in the headlights. At that point my memory goes fragile. There is some quick slippery violence, and the farm boy is on his knees. Jack Ray is standing above him, waiting, wheezing as he breathes.

It's over, everybody knows, and soon it is. Two more grunting punches, and the farm boy is down again, and Jack Ray steps back, his eyes gone soft and almost bewildered in the light as a little shudder moves through the crowd, and someone shouts, and the bottles pass again. I see Jack Ray, there in those headlights, smiling like a child now that it's finished, the farm boy up on his knees, shaking his head.

No harm done, the air clear. I see it over and over, summer dance after summer dance. I see the kind of heroism my boyhood educated me to understand and respect.

And I hate the part that comes next. I grew up and ran the haying and combine crews on our ranch, and there eventually came a time when I hired Jack Ray to work for me. He had worked a lot of seasons for my father, and such men always had a job with us. Jack was maybe fifty by that time and crippled by his life, the magic gone, a peaceable man who seemed to have turned a little simple. He did what he could, chores around the cookhouse, and once in a while he drank. After a bout in town that earned him some time in the county jail, he would show up grinning in the bunkhouse.

"Well, hell, Jack," I would say, "it's a new day."

"Kid," he would say, "she's a new world every morning."

Looking backward is one of our main hobbies here in the American West, as we age. And we are aging, which could mean we are growing up. Or not. It's a difficult process for a culture that has always been so insistently boyish. Jack Ray has been dead a long time now. As my father said, he drank his liver right into the ground. "But, by God," my father said, "he was something once."

∽

Possibility is the oldest American story. Head west for freedom and the chance of inventing a spanking new life for yourself. Our citizens are always leaping the traces when their territory gets too small and cramped.

Back in the late 1950s living with my wife and our small

children in our little cattle-ranch house, when things would get too tight on a rainy Sunday afternoon in November I always had the excuse of work. "I got to go out," I would say, and I would duck away to the peacefulness of driving the muddy fields and levee banks in my old Ford pickup. Or, if the roads were too bad, I would go down to the blacksmith shop and bang on some damned thing.

Whenever I find myself growing grim about the mouth; whenever it is damp, drizzly November in my soul; whenever I find myself involuntarily pausing before coffin warehouses, and bringing up the rear of every funeral I meet. . . . Then he runs away to sea. *Ishmael.*

". . . lighting out for territory," says Huckleberry Finn, with his brokenhearted optimism, right at the end of his getaway down the Mississippi.

And it wasn't just the runaway boys in books. John Colter left Ohio at the age of thirty, to head up the Missouri with Lewis and Clark in 1804. He stayed west another five years, earning his keep as a fur trapper in pursuit of the beaver. One fearsome Montana winter he took a legendary walk from Fort Lisa on the Yellowstone, traveling through what is Yellowstone Park to circumnavigate the Tetons—about a thousand miles on snowshoes through country where no white man had ever been before. A thing both wondrous and powerful drove him. Maybe it was a need so simple as being out, away.

Imagine those shining snowy mountains burning against the sheltering endless bowl of clean sky, and Colter alone there in Jackson Hole. We will not see such things again, not any of us, ever. It's gone. We know it is. Only one man ever got to be Colter. Not even Bridger or Joe Meek or Jedediah Smith had a world so absolutely to themselves. Except for some natives, who maybe never thought they were alone.

In 1836 Narcissa and Marcus Whitman came west with Eliza and Henry Spalding. The first white women had crossed the Rockies. Along the way they witnessed one of the last fur-trapper rendezvous, on the Green River in Wyoming. Think of those Presbyterian women among the inhabitants of wilderness. Less than ten years later Marcus Whitman was leading one of the first wagon trains west from St. Louis to Oregon country.

The New York newspaper editor Horace Greeley worried about the exodus, wondering what those families could be seeking, leaving behind the best of climates and agricultural lands, schools and churches and markets: "For what, then, do they brave the desert, the wilderness, the savage, the snowy precipices of the Rocky Mountains, the early summer march, the storm-drenched bivouac, and the gnawings of famine? Only to fulfill their destiny! There is probably not one among them whose outward circumstances will be improved by this perilous pilgrimage."

Anybody sensible, Greeley suggested, would stop "... this side of the jumping-off place." The only practice stupider than such migration, he said, was suicide.

It's easy to understand his puzzlement. The wagon trains were predominantly middle-class ventures. Poor folks couldn't afford a wagon, much less provisions. The basic outfitting cost up toward a thousand dollars. And in those long-gone days that was some real money. But seemingly sensible people persisted in selling their good farms and heading west.

Imagine half the population of Ohio picking up sticks, selling out, and heading for one of our latter-day mythological frontiers, Alaska or Australia. Greeley was right, it was crazy, it was a mania.

What was pushing them? Lots of things. Among them a quite legitimate fear of mortal corruption and death.

Cholera. By the spring of 1849 an epidemic had reached St. Louis. Ten percent of the population died of the disease. The road west from Independence was likened to traveling through a graveyard.

But mostly, we have to believe, they were lured west by promises. Promises of paradise for the taking. Free land, crystalline water, great herds of game roaming the natural meadowlands, good fishing, gold, all in unfettered abundance, a new world every morning.

What compelled men to believe promises of paradise on earth with such simpleminded devotion? Well, for openers, a gut yearning for the chance of becoming someone else, and freedom from the terrible weight of responsibilities, freedom too often equalling free, without cost.

My own great-grandfather on my father's side left Michigan in 1849 to travel down the Mississippi and across to Panama, where he hiked west through the jungles on the route Balboa had blazed and caught a ship north to California and the gold camps. After a long and bootless career of chasing mineral trace in the mountain streams, first in the central Sierra and then up around the foothills of Mount Shasta, he gave it up and turned to ranching and school teaching in one place after another around the Northwest, until in 1897 he died white-trash poor in the sagebrush backlands near Silver Lake, Oregon, leaving a family determined to shake his suicidal despair.

It wasn't just the gold that he never found—such instant-boomer riches were to have been only the beginning. The green and easy dreamland fields of some home place were to have been the ultimate reward for his searching, the grape arbor beside the white house he would own outright, where he could rest out some last serene years while the hordes of grandchildren played down across the lawns by the sod-banked pond where the tame ducks swam and fed and squawked in their happy, idiot way. The pastoral heaven on this earth—some particular secret and heart's-desire version of it—has time and again proved to be the absolute heart in American dreams. All this we promise you.

Childhood, it has been said, is always partly a lie of poetry. When I was maybe eight years old, in the fall of the year, I would have to go out in the garden after school with damp burlap sacks and cover the long rows of cucumber and tomato plants, so they wouldn't freeze.

It was a hated, cold-handed job that had to be done every evening. I daydreamed along in a halfhearted, distracted way, flopping the sacks onto the plants, sorry for myself and angry because I was alone at my boring work. No doubt my younger brother and sister were in the house and warm. Eating cookies.

But then a great strutting bird appeared out from the dry remnants of our corn, black tail feathers flaring and a monstrous yellow-orange air sac pulsating from its white breast, its throat croaking with popping sounds like rust in a joint.

The bird looked to be stalking me with grave slow intensity, coming after me from a place I could not understand as real, and yet quite recognizable, the sort of terrifying creature that would sometimes spawn in the incoherent world of my night-dreams. In my story, now, I say it looked like death, come to say hello. Then, it was simply an apparition.

The moment demanded all my boyish courage, but I stood my ground, holding one of those wet sacks out before me like a shield, stepping slowly backwards, listening as the terrible creature croaked, its bright preposterous throat pulsating—and then the great bird flapped its wings in an angry way, raising a little commonplace dust.

It was the dust, I think, that did it, convincing me that this could not be a dream. My fear collapsed, and I felt foolish as I understood this was a creature I had heard my father talk about, a courting sage-grouse, we called them prairie chickens. This was only a bird and not much interested in me at all. But for an instant it had been both phantom and real, the thing I deserved, come to punish me for my anger.

For that childhood moment I believed the world to be absolutely inhabited by an otherness that was utterly demonic and natural, not of my own making. But soon as that bird was enclosed in a story that defined it as a commonplace prairie chicken, I was no longer frightened. It is a skill we learn early, the art of inventing stories to explain away the fearful sacred strangeness of the world. Storytelling and make-believe, like war and agriculture, are among the arts of self-defense, and all of them are ways of enclosing otherness and claiming ownership.

Such emblematic memories continue to surface, as I grow older and find ways to accept them into the fiction of myself. One of the earliest, from a time before I ever went to school, is of studying the worn oiled softwood flooring in the Warner Valley store where my mother took me when she picked up the mail three times a week. I have no idea how many years that floor had been tromped and dirtied and swept, but by the time I recall it was worn into a topography of swales and buttes, traffic patterns and hard knots, much like the land, if you will, under the wear of a glacier. For a child, as his mother gossiped with the postmistress, it was a place, high ground and valleys, prospects and sanctuaries, and I in my boredom could invent stories about it—finding a coherency I loved, a place that was mine. They tore up that floor somewhere around the time I started school, and I had the sense to grieve.

The coherency I found worn into those floorboards was mirrored a few years later, just before the war began, when I was seven or eight, in the summertime play of my brother and sister and cousins and myself, as we laid out roads to drive and rectangular fields to work with our toy trucks in the dirt under the huge old box elder, which also functioned as a swing tree near the kitchen door to our house. It was a little play world we made for ourselves, and it was, we believed, just like the vast world beyond. In it we imitated the kind of ordering we watched each spring while our father laid out the garden with such measured precision, and the kind of planning we could not help but sense while riding with him along the levee banks in his dusty Chevrolet pickup truck. All the world we knew was visible from the front porch of our house, inside the valley, and all the work he did was directed toward making it orderly, functional, and productive—and of course that work seemed sacred.

Our play ended when a small rattlesnake showed up in our midst, undulating in sweeping little curving lines across our dusty make-believe fields. A young woman who cooked for my mother killed the snake in a matter-of-fact way with a shovel. But the next spring my mother insisted, and my father hauled in topsoil and planted the packed dirt, where we had played at our toylike world of fields, into a lawn where rattlesnakes would never come. We hated him for it.

These stories suggest reasons why, during childhood winters through the Second World War, such an important segment of my imagination lived amid maps of Europe and the Pacific. Maps delineated the dimensions of that dream which was the war for me, maps and traced drawings of aircraft camouflaged for combat. I collected them like peacetime city boys collect baseball cards, and I colored them in with crayons, my far South Pacific and Europe invaded and shaped by dreams and invisible forces I could not hope to make sense of any other way.

⚮

In the spring of 1942, just before I turned ten years old, we opened every first-period class in our one-room Warner Valley schoolhouse singing, "Praise the Lord and Pass the Ammunition." We embraced the war. We heard it every morning on the Hallicrafters Trans-Oceanic radio, while we got ready for school, and during recess we ran endless games of gunfighter pursuit and justifiably merciless death in the playgrounds. Mostly we killed Hitler and Mister Tojo.

Fall down, you're dead.

When it came your turn to play Nazi, you were honor bound to eventually fall killed through the long adult agony, twisting and staggering to heedless collapse in the dirt. Out in our landlocked, end-of-the-road, rancher valley, the air was bright and clean with purpose.

Always, at least in memory, those running battles involve my cousins and my younger brother and my even younger sister, and a black-and-white dog named Victory. Out back of the house in the summer of 1942 we circled and shot our ways through groves of wild plum in heavy fruit, and we swung to ambush from gnarled limbs in the apple orchard where the blue flies and the yellowjackets were mostly interested in having their way with the rotting fallen fruit: yellowjackets flitting to a hive in the hollow trunk of a Lombardy poplar along the irrigation ditch, burning the air with their going, and near to the secret, stinging, irreligious heart of *my* paradise.

⚮

In late September our dog named Victory was crushed under the rear duals of a semi-truck flatbed hauling 100-

pound burlap sacks of my father's newly combined oats across 40 twisting miles of gravel road over the Warner Mountains to town and the railroad. My sister ran shrieking to the kitchen door, and my mother came to the roadside in her apron, and I was stoic and tough-minded as that poor animal panted and died. *Beyond the crystal sea, undreamed shores, precious angels.*

This was a time when our national life was gone to war against U-boats and the Bataan Death March, betrayal reeking everywhere. The death of that dog with cockleburrs matted into his coat must have shimmered with significance past heartbreak. We were American and proud, and we were steeled to deal with these matters.

So we unearthed a shallow grave in the good loam soil at the upper end of the huge rancher garden my father laid out each spring in those days, before it became cheaper to feed our crews from truckloads of canned goods bought wholesale in the cities. We gathered late-blooming flowers from the border beneath my mother's bedroom window, we loaded the stiffening carcass of that dead dog on a red wagon, and we staged a funeral with full symbolic honors.

My older cousin blew taps through his fist, my brother hid his face, and my six-year-old sister wept openly, which was all right since she was a little child. I waved a leafy bough of willow over the slope-sided grave while my other cousins shoveled the loose dry soil down on the corpse.

It is impossible to know what the child who was myself felt, gazing east across the valley that I can still envision so clearly—the ordered garden and the sage-covered slope running down to the slough-cut meadows of the Thompson Field, willows there concealing secret hideaway places where I would burrow away from the world for hours, imagining I was some animal, hidden and watching the stock cows graze the open islands of meadow grass.

On the far side of the valley lay the great level distances of the plow-ground fields that had so recently been tule swamps, reaching to the rise of barren eastern ridges. That enclosed valley is the home I imagine walking when some-day I fall into the dream that is my death. My real, particular, vivid and populated solace for that irrevocable moment of utter loss when the mind stops forever. The chill of that re-membered September evening feels right as I imagine that heartbreakingly distant boy.

It's hard for me to know where I got the notion of waving that willow branch over our burial of that poor dog unless I find it in this other memory, from about the same time. A Paiute girl of roughly my own age died of measles in the ramshackle encampment her people maintained alongside the irrigation ditch that eventually led to our vast garden. A dozen or so people lived there, and true or not, I keep thinking of them as in touch with some remnant memories of hunting and gathering forebears who summered so many generations in the valley we had so recently come to own.

In the fall of 1890 a man named James Mooney went west under the auspices of the Bureau of Ethnology to investigate the rise of Native American religious fervor that culminated in the massacre at Wounded Knee on December 29. In Mooney's report, *The Ghost Dance Religion and the Sioux Outbreak of 1890*, there is a statement delivered by a Paiute man named Captain Dick at Fort Bidwell in Surprise Valley—right in the home territory I am talking about, at the junction on maps where California and Nevada come together at the Oregon border.

All Indians must dance, everywhere, keep on danc-ing. Pretty soon in the next spring Big Man come.

He bring back game of every kind. The game be
thick everywhere. All dead Indians come back
and live again. They all be strong just like young
men, be young again. Old blind Indians see again
and get young and have fine time. When the Old
Man comes this way, then all the Indians go to the
mountains, high up away from the whites. Whites
can't hurt the Indians then. Then while Indians way
up high, big flood comes like water and all white
people die, get drowned. After that water go away
and then nobody but Indians everywhere game all
kinds thick. Then medicine man tell Indians to send
word to all Indians to keep up dancing and the good
time will come. Indians who don't dance, who don't
believe in this word, will grow little, just about a foot
high, and stay that way. Some of them will turn into
wood and will be burned in the fire.

In the 1950s and 1960s a Paiute named Conlan Dick lived
in a cabin on our ranch in Warner Valley and helped to look
after the irrigation and fences. Conlan was reputed to be
a kind of medicine man in our local mythology, related to
the man who delivered that statement. His wife, whose
name I cannot recall, did ironing for women in the valley.
And there was a son, a young man named Virgil Dick, who
sometimes came to Warner for a few weeks and helped his
father with the fieldwork.

In the early 1960s my cousin, the one who blew taps
through his fist in 1942, was riding horseback across the
swampy spring meadows alongside Conlan. He asked if
Virgil was Conlan's only child.

Conlan grinned. "Naw," he said. "But you know, those
kids, they play outside, and they get sick and they die."

Story after story. Is it possible to claim that proceeding

through some incidents in this free-associative manner is in fact a technique, a way of discovery? Probably. One of our model narrators these days is the patient spinning and respinning the past and trying to resolve it into a story that makes sense.

". . . they get sick and they die." Once I had the romance in me to think that this was the mature comment of a man who had grown up healed into wholeness and connection with the ways of nature to a degree I would never understand. Now I think it was more likely the statement of a man trying to forget his wounds—so many of which were inflicted by school-yard warriors like us. A healthy culture could never have taught him to forego sorrow.

In any event, Captain Dick's magic was dead.

All these stories are part of my own story about a place called Home, and a time in which I imagined we owned it all. The girl who died was named Pearl. I recall her name with that particular exactness which occasionally hovers in memories. She was of enormous interest to us because she so obviously disdained our foolish play with make-believe weapons and miniature trucks. Or so it seemed. Maybe she was only shy or had been warned away from us. But to our minds she lived with adults and shared in the realities of adult lives in ways we did not, and now she was being paid the attention of burial.

Try to imagine their singing that spring morning. I cannot. I like to think our running brigade of warrior children might have been touched by dim sorrow-filled wailing in the crystalline brightness of her morning, but the memory is silent.

Maybe it's enough to recall the sight of people she loved, carrying her elaborately clothed body in an open home-built casket. Not that we saw it up close, or that we ever really saw a body, clothed or unclothed.

They were making their slow parade up a sandy path through the sagebrush to her burial in the brushy plot, loosely fenced with barbed wire, which we knew as the "Indian Graveyard." I see them high on the banking sand-hill behind our house, and beyond them the abrupt 2,000-foot lift of rimrock that forms the great western lip of our Warner Valley. That rim is always there, the table of lava-flow at the top breaking so abruptly, dropping through long scree-slopes clustered with juniper. As I grow older it is always at my back. The sun sets there, summer and winter. I can turn and squint my eyes and see it.

From the flowering trees in the homesteader's orchard behind our house we watched that astonishing processional through my father's binoculars, and then we ran out through the brush beyond the garden, tasting the perfect spring morning and leaping along the small animal trails, filled with thrilling purpose, and silent and urgent. We had to be closer.

The procession was just above us on the sandy trail when we halted, those people paying us no mind but frightening us anyway, mourning men and women in their dark castaway clothing and bright blankets and strange robes made of animal skins, clutching at spring blossoms and sweeping at the air with thick sheaves of willow in new leaf. It is now that I would like to hear the faint singsong of their chanting. I would like to think we studied them through the dancing waves of oncoming heat, and found in them the only models we had ever had for such primal ceremonies.

But this keeps becoming fiction. Ours was a rising class of agricultural people, new to that part of the world, too preoccupied with an endless ambition toward perfection in their work to care at all for any tradition of religion. No one in our immediate families had ever died, and no one ever would so far as we knew. None of us, in those days, had any interest in religion or ritual.

So I have this story of those shrouded people proceeding through my imagination. I feel them celebrating as that young girl entered into the ripe fruit of another paradise, lamenting the dole-food exigencies of their own lives, some of them likely thinking she was lucky to have escaped.

But I don't really have much idea what was going on behind the story I've made of that morning. It was is if those people were trailing along that sandy path toward tomorrow land themselves. Some of them, somewhere, are likely still alive.

In a book called *Shoshone*, the poet Ed Dorn tells of interviewing an ancient man and woman in a trailer house on the Duck Valley Reservation, a couple of hundred miles east of us but still deep in the high basin and range desert, along the border between Idaho and Nevada. They were both more than one hundred years old and told Dorn they had never heard of white men until past the age of thirty. Which is possible.

It's easy to imagine those ancient people grinning in what looks to be a toothless old way in their aluminum-sided trailer house, with screens on the windows, on the Duck Valley Reservation. They must have understood the value of stories. Dorn says they demanded cartons of cigarettes before they allowed themselves to be photographed. The point is, they were willing to be part of any make-believe anybody could invent for them, willing to tell their stories and let us make of them what we could. But not for nothing. Stories are valuable precisely to the degree that they are for the moment useful in our ongoing task of finding coherency in the world, and those old people must have known that whatever story Dorn was imagining was worth at least the price of some smokes.

My father's Cat skinners bulldozed the shacktown Indian camp with its willow-roofed ramada into a pile of old posts and lumber and burned it, after the last of those people had gone to wherever they went. Our children? In the fall of 1942, the same year that girl named Pearl was buried, they learned something about the emotional thrust of a warrior code as the news from Hallicrafters Trans-Oceanic radio was translated into singing in first-period music class, and they loaded that dead dog named Victory in a red wagon and trailed him toward burial at the upper end of the garden. And I waved sweeps of willow over the ceremony while my cousin blew taps through his fist.

Buckaroos

THIS IS A STRING OF STORIES about a land of empire ranches: the IL and the Whitehorse, the MC and the ZX and Peter French's great P Ranch. History in that country is partly the story of those ranches and cattle and the great horsemen, but it is more accurately focused on getting the work done, feeding cattle from a creaking hay wagon while snow blows level to the ground in late January.

My education in such realities began with men like Ross Dollarhide, who lived to see ninety years and died in bed, having endured. The MC, where I was raised, was like a feudal kingdom in those days, not many neighbors you ever encountered, nobody around for the most part but our family and the people who worked for them. Our world was utterly centered on horses and cattle in those years before the end of World War II, 1945, when everybody went to pickup trucks and tractors. We lost the farm, an old man told me, when we went to the goddamned tractors.

That desert country in southeastern Oregon and northern Nevada still is an enclave of unsettled territory, lava-rock and sagebrush flats, fault-block mountains, and swampy land-locked valleys echoing with the calls of white pelicans and sandhill cranes and Canada geese and thousands of ducks like the green-winged teal and the redheads and canvasbacks nobody sees so often anymore.

Amid such empty distances expansive personalities are commonplace.

Children grew up addicted to running their horses, as I did, a manifestation of spirit that adults claimed to see as a disease (even if they themselves once in a while staged a race). A horse, I was told, was not a toy.

My cousins and I grew up understanding that horses were creatures with their own complex sensibilities, which could not only be broken (that name for training) but spoiled—ruined—by cheap-shit frivolity such as pointless galloping—a boy coming heedlessly along a country road with his horse in a lather.

But we were the children of the people who owned the ranches and could sometimes get away with things, so I listened to what I was told but galloped anyway, down long secret lanes through the willows and sloughs, before sunup in the endlessness of midsummer, on my way to visit the hay camps where the old men in the round corrals were lassoing their buck-rake teams.

Then, in 1940, the summer I turned eight years old, an older cousin and I were deemed big enough to be useful and sent to ride with my grandfather's crew of buckaroos on the sea of desert east of the ranch, where our family summered their thousands of mother cows.

What a thing it was to be a child, watching those men step onto a spooky stocking-footed traveling horse in the light of early morning and knowing you were expected to keep up for the rest of the day. My cousin and I weren't much use that summer and most of the next (I was learning things like, never cry). But we grew and toughened as boys will. By 1943 we were, we thought, almost cowhands. We learned to shoe our own horses and braid rawhide on rainy days and to travel for hours like grown-ups, at a long trot.

We were near the end of secret galloping; we were becoming little men.

Ross Dollarhide was wagon boss for the MC buckaroo outfit. He was in charge of the riders, a cook, chuck wagon, and sixty-five or seventy head of horses in the remuda while looking after the Hereford cows and their calves that my grandfather was summering in the desert. And maybe 500 head of bulls, purebreds, from places like Wyoming and Montana, shipped in on the railroad. There was no chance of inbreeding.

Dollarhide was as nearly as old as my grandfather, and he was my main example of how to live like a man in the world. He'd been a legend since he rode into the Whitehorse Ranch on a fat-tired bicycle the summer he was sixteen, around 1900, and announced he was looking for work, riding rough horses if there was a choice. According to legend, the old hands grinned and put him up on some Roman-nosed gray stud nobody had even thought about trying to ride. We know the rest: that devil horse bucked down to a stalled and sweaty, bloody-mouthed froth—even rode to death in some versions of the fireside tale—and young Dollarhide was triumphant as the old-timers shook their heads and smiled.

"We got one," they would say. "A real one." He was a real one to us kids, all those years later, for sure. We all believed some version of that story. Dollarhide was a great horseman, and he had earned and deserved any esteem the world might grant. We rode out each morning behind a legendary man, and we knew it. At least I did, when I was thirteen.

∽

You had to stay playful to survive. That was another thing we were taught, by clear example, watching the men around us, in whom a certain childish recklessness (at least in the best of them, the finest hands) had never died.

Then one burning afternoon that playfulness got us crossways. There for a moment we left that buckaroo crew afoot, without horses, like fools.

Just at daybreak one bright morning in June while we were rolling our beds, making ready to move the four-horse chuck wagon from the mountainside camp at Ackley to Sagehen Spring, my cousin and I were detailed to help the wrango boy move the seventy some odd saddle horses in the MC remuda. Once we'd turned them out of the willow corral at Ackley they'd be ours as we herded them twenty miles down country across the alkaline flats to the fenced-in field where the wet-weather creek at Sagehen got lost in tall brush. There wasn't much at Sagehen, no sign of a house, just a hog-wire corral and field built of rusty barbed wire and crooked juniper posts. That corral was a small target in a vast territory (nowadays there's a highway just south of Sagehen Spring; in those days there were almost no internal-combustion engines in that country). We were to take it easy. What we were to do was graze the herd on Ackley Mountain through the morning and then ease them on down to Sagehen in the late afternoon.

It was clear: if we got those horses running with their heads, and lost control of them, there wasn't a fence to turn them within fifty miles. An old hand, Merle Dodson, went along, to keep an eye on us.

What is there to say about Merle Dodson? He was known as "Tarzan," a barroom tag given him because he was, according to my father when I asked him years later, close to animal if he was drinking. He was huge-handed and barrel-chested, stronger than he knew, impossible to wound, nobody to fight as strangers had found out any number of times, but he was always willing and happy to be entertained.

"That damned Tarz," people would say. "If he ain't something, you tell me, what is?" What he was on this day was full of vinegar when we eased our drifty grazing herd of bay horses, all of them geldings, over the crest of Ackley Mountain to encounter the mustangs who were also drifting along in their shaggy spotted-horse way.

There were maybe twenty or so mustangs, mares and colts, a half-dozen branded geldings that had got away from some ranch or another in the long-ago past, and no doubt a stud horse even if I don't recall any such creature. What I recall is the way we let them drift into the remuda and mix, the way we fell in after them; I recall running horses.

"We're mustanging," Tarz Dodson whispered. Something like that. It was his plan. It frightened us, but we never thought of refusing.

Besides, if I learned something that day, which is the point of this story, it had nothing to do with caution, but rather with the splendor of running with the wind. That was the lesson of the summer.

We were going to ease our great herd of horses along the road slow as we could through the afternoon, then stir them into a long run just at the end, and turn them into the corral at Sagehen Spring before they came to any sense of what was happening. We were going to have those mustangs inside fences before they realized they had been trapped. We were going to own those mustangs. That was Tarz Dodson's idea; the whole buckaroo crew could turn some money on the side. It wasn't a plan my grandfather would have endorsed.

I have no idea what those remnant animals were worth at that time. Their herds grew during World War II, when their natural predators, young cowhands, were off to war.

After the war they were cleaned out of that country, run with airplanes and rounded up in swirling herds; most of them eventually shot and processed into chicken feed.

We brought it off, my cousin and I and the MC wrango boy and Tarz Dodson; we got the mustangs folded into our herd, running with the remuda. At Sagehen we circled the entire herd moving in a great sweep through the afternoon while somebody got the corral gate open. It was about then when I realized something was very wrong.

The chuck-wagon tent was up, and everybody on the crew had turned their horses loose into the field. Our horses were it; lose the herd and everybody but us was afoot, which was no joke in that wide open country, sure as hell not in a buckaroo outfit. Old Man Dollarhide was out front of that chuck-wagon tent with a coffee cup in his hand, studying our act like an old eagle contemplating a final kill.

We hit that corral gate perfectly. Those mustangs circled maybe twice, then went out the other side, scattering hog-wire. They circled the field a time or two and went right on through that fence like ghosts with the MC remuda following. The running horses were flowering out into freedom and starting to spill off in all directions, and there was nothing we could do because we were still back trying to get through the corral gate.

What I remember is some man took my horse, leaping up into my short-legged saddle, and another took my cousin's horse. What had seemed like play was abruptly ended. Hours later they came back driving a remnant of the remuda before them. This was serious, a disgrace; the story would get out; the MC buckaroo crew would be the laughing stock of the country.

What I remember is standing around the cook fire like a fool. Tarz Dodson was fired and rode off into the night with his bedroll behind his saddle. But what matters most to me is the feeling I took from those moments as that herd of running horses turned in their sweep toward the corral at Sagehen—a sense of triumphant release. No more the child.

Maybe I got my ass whipped, but I don't think so. I don't think those men ever touched me. They taught me to never give a major shit about small change, an operative principle in my good moments ever since. I had been along on a big ride, and I was part of a story that would be told and laughed about in country taverns for years, even by Dollarhide and Tarz Dodson. In that if nothing else, I was like those men who were, at least occasionally, the real item.

One sure thing about us boys on those old dust-eating summery afternoons during World War II, out there branding MC calves on the high deserts, we dreamed of lost old highways and rodeos. But that country is like a hidden kingdom. Change and escape do not come easy.

Owyhee. Sounds like Hawaii. In 1819 Donald Mackenzie brought one of the first brigades of fur trappers into the Snake River country. He came from the mouth of the Columbia, and he brought with him a few Hawaiians. He sent them off to explore the uncharted river that came into the Snake from the south, through the desert barrens. The Hawaiians never came back. The river and territory inherited their name.

This is the story of going back, in 1980, on the road seeking romance and Hawaiians in the desert. What I wanted was Nevada, and *laissez-faire,* hard-way sixes at four in the morning and then, if it should suit my fancy, a quiet drink on the terrace with myself and the sunrise, like a grown-up in the land where everybody gets to do what they want to do, anyway, part of the time.

I was heading to visit the chuck-wagon buckaroo outfit run by the IL Ranch, on the edge of the Owyhee desert north of Tuscarora, Nevada. The IL was then an outfit run in the old and sensible way, horses pulling the chuck wagon, and no trucks and no town cars and the no horse trailers—men and livestock and the countryside settling into a routine with one another amid the terms of the season.

The first branding of the spring was to be the next morning, if the weather cleared. The smell of branding was one of the wistful things I had come looking for. But the storms had been driving in from the west, spitting snow and rain, and the prospects did not look good. Hot branding irons scald and blot on the hides of wet calves.

Fearful that the trip would be all muddy roads and bad news, I skipped the Tuscarora turnoff and went on into Elko, one of those two-hearted Nevada ranching and gambling towns that grew up at the end of the nineteenth century after the Union Pacific traced the route of California-bound wagon trains along the Humboldt River. Up on the hill, in the shade of box elder, country people mow their lawns and read the *Western Horseman* magazine on their patios while down by the interstate there's gambling and bars that never close, and always, off on the exotic edges of what I knew from high school, the dangerous reek of prostitution.

The whorehouses put me in a you-can't-go-home again quandary of the most elemental kind. Back in the misty past there is this land inhabited by dreams and passions, and you love it—your daddy was rich and your momma good looking—and you want it to be all perfection, bronzed in your memory like baby shoes. And whorehouses, well, I just don't know.

There was a time I liked them fine. In Klamath Falls, Oregon, where we wintered when I was in high school, there were five houses, places with names like the Iron

Door and the Palm Hotel. There was a crowd of us growing boys who ruined our athletic careers by hanging out in
those homes for the misbegotten Eros of the times. Say it's
a Friday night in February and the basketball game is over,
and the alternative is the sock hop down at the Teen Age
Club—lots of leaning against the wall and studying your
look-alike basketball rivals from out of town while the girls
dance with one another. Pretty soon somebody nods in a
cool-eyed way, and you and your fellows all drift down to
the Iron Door.

And there were summers, over in Lakeview, Oregon,
near the ranch. Riding with the wagon on the desert, or
working in the hayfields, I was earning a man's wages by the
time I was fifteen, and summers were a different ball game.
Out beyond the rodeo grounds there was a district called
Hollywood. It was official—the houses paid taxes into a
special city fund for streetlights. This was part of the time-
less rationale you would hear, the basic argument having to
do with ensuring the safety of decent women. Sex-crazed
ranch hands could work out their primitive lusts down in
Hollywood and not wander the streets molesting wives
and mothers. And besides, how about those streetlights?
Hollywood, I guess, was a kind of a civic sacrifice area.

The girls, some not much older than we were, would
serve us boys with whiskey and take our money and smile
and laugh with us so long as we could pay our way. Those
houses sided with tar paper were not places to contemplate
romance or running away with your darling, but they were
where so many of us received our most formidable training
for manhood. We learned the most central message of our
culture: do not break your heart over anything like promis-
cuity; property remains. It was the message my grandfather
turned out to have been teaching me all of my life.

In 1980, in my Elko motel room, sipping at a pint bottle

of Jack Daniel's whiskey, I could not bring myself to drift back down to the cathouses. Like Hemingway said in another context, and he is our patron in these matters, ". . . the war was always there, but we did not go to it any more."

All of it, in Elko, was like coming home. In the J. M. Capriola Company on Commercial Street I wandered around just touching the gear, rawhide riatas and horsehair mecates, rubbing my hands over working buckaroo saddles, eyeing the silver-mounted Garcia spurs and Spanish bits and belt buckles in their glass cases, feeling a pang of awe at the way prices had gone up. At Capriola's, a complete gear-up for a desert-horseback working man—saddle, bridle, Spanish and snaffle bits, chinks (the chaps they wear in the buckaroo north country, cut off at the knee), tepee camp tent, hobbles plus a pair of woolly sheepskin chaps for winter, bedroll and blankets—cost a load of money for a working cowhand, even if he got board and room free. But the gear is built to accompany a working person through a good many seasons of serious endeavor, up and down the road.

Downstairs in the Commercial Hotel were the crap tables and the mounted upright figure of what is reputed to be the largest white polar bear ever killed, by native hunters off Point Hope, Alaska. At midnight the Commercial was Point Hope for everybody, at least in fantasy. If you could cloud your mind, you could write off a run of bad karma in the midst of hard-way sixes, which was the art I was practicing, along about midnight in Elko, the land of the free.

So when morning dawned bright, rain clouds gone, I was ready for my trip out past Tuscarora to the IL. For me it was like going back in time. The headquarters of the IL Ranch is on the Owyhee South Fork, edged up on the sage hills above about 2,500 acres of native meadow hayland. Off west is the enormous flatland of the Owyhee desert, elevation always over 5,000 feet, reaching to the Santa Rosa

Mountains, 70 miles away by air, over 9,000 feet and snow-covered in mid-May. About 20 miles east there's Jack's Peak, rising 10,000 feet in the Independence Mountains over the Columbia Basin, where the IL cattle and sheep run during the late summer and early fall.

If Elko smelled like home, this *was* home. Down in a cramped office next to the cookhouse I met the ranch boss, Bill Maupin, and his wife, Wanda, and the sheep boss, Allen King, who was up from the sheep range, which is on the south side of the Humboldt River, far to the west between Battle Mountain and Winnemucca.

The IL ran about 5,000 mother cows and another 5,000 head of sheep on about 480,000 acres of deeded and government-leased land. And it was the smallest of major spreads in that country. The Petan Ranch to the north, the Spanish Ranch, over in the Independence Valley northeast of Tuscarora, and the Garvey Ranch to the west in Paradise Valley—they were all bigger, at least by reputation.

It's regarded as rude to ask a man how much property he owns. But there's a story about a man named John G. Taylor, who was an early owner of the IL. Seems he was tired of hearing about the Miller and Lux string of ranches. Around 1900 it was claimed a man could ride from Burns in Oregon to the south end of the San Joaquin Valley in California and camp every night but one on Miller and Lux land. "Damn, I don't know about that," John G. Taylor is supposed to have said, "but I know this. I can walk on the backs of my own sheep from Lovelock to the three forks of the Owyhee River." That would be maybe 150 miles.

A buckaroo at the IL drew not much money, but board and all the room he wanted for his bedroll. Hard work and you had to respect it if you wanted the job. But it was a life to which a lot of people, in a complex variety of ways, were returning. Turning back to livestock and the long wheel of days, and some chance at self-knowledge, or at least some knowledge of who killed the cow you were eating.

On the way to where the IL wagon crew was branding, about twenty miles west from headquarters, Bill Maupin pointed out the ruins of an old stone house sitting grand and alone alongside a wet-weather creek. The story is that a Mormon man built it around 1900 and brought his three wives to live there. Two of the wives died that winter, and he buried them in the basement, since all the ground outside was frozen hard as metal. The joke was that those women were winter-killed.

She is a wonderful country, go the intimations, but a good place to be careful every chance you get. If you are going alone—into your radical mountain-man independence and isolation and loneliness—think ahead and take precautions. Winter-killed brings to mind another charmed saying: "She is a hard country on women and horses." Which means, I guess, that men and mules can make out all right and have a swell time digging graves in the basement?

This country fosters a kind of woman who never seems to bother about who she is supposed to be, mainly because there is always work, and getting it done in a level-eyed way is what counts most. Getting the work done, on horseback or not, and dicing their troubles into jokes. These women wind up looking fifty when they are thirty-seven and fifty-three when they are seventy. It's as though they wear down to what counts and just last there, fine and staring the devil in the eye every morning.

Bill Maupin pointed out a place near the edge of a sandy wash through the sagebrush where a dead man had been found with three silver dollars in his pocket. One morning, the fellow, dead of natural causes from what anybody could tell, was sitting in a buggy, his horses standing; his white eyes were open to the new sun. The sheriff came out from

Elko, looked him over, and blessed him. They buried him where they found him with the three shining silver dollars in his pocket for luck. The country is thick with such stories. Unknown travelers.

Bill Maupin and I grew up knowing a lot of the same people, surely the same kind of people. The cow boss at the IL, Tom Anderson, turned out to be a man I had missed knowing when we were both younger. Tom broke in buckarooing on the MC just after I went away to the Air Force, when Hugh Cahill was running the MC wagon.

In this memory, our kid is maybe eleven years old. The remuda would circle in one of those stone corrals, and the alkaline dust would lift in a clearing string to the blooming bowl of sky. I was learning responsibility.

My grandfather, during the hard times of the Great Depression, had yielded to one of those dreams and staked the property he spent a lifetime accumulating in order to get his hands on the MC in Warner Valley, east of Lakeview: some 21,000 acres of peat-soil swamplands in the valley and what seemed in those horseback days to be endless summer range east on the desert. A million or so acres, that desert range was mostly Taylor grazing land leased from the federal government, but my grandfather treated it as if it were his own.

Before the end of World War II there was no asphalt within thity-five miles of headquarters on the MC. No telephones; a Delco generator for electricity. A great deal of time was spent talking to yourself in the company of animals.

Which was fine. You would slow down and get used to the pace. *Going to the desert*—that's what we called summering out there with the cattle—ten or so riders, a chuck wagon and cook and no automobiles. Clevon Dixon, who was cow boss on the MC in the 1960s, said the quiet just took you over.

"First week," he'd say, "I always hate it, wondering what's happening somewhere. Second week I don't care so much. After that I can't imagine anyplace else, and I don't ever want go back to town. If it wasn't for winter, you could stay out there forever."

Anyway, there I was, eleven years old, learning the business. It was late June, and we were branding calves alongside an alkaline sink on the Gooch Plateau, right near the Oregon/Nevada border.

We had gathered maybe a hundred range cows and their spring calves out of the low hills off south, driven them down across a lava-rock flat, built a fire of greasewood and sage to heat the MC irons, and we were just getting started. A couple of ropers, Dollarhide among them, would ride to the herd and hind-foot the calves with their tight-woven rawhide riatas and drag them to the fire where three or four of the strong young bucks were doing the groundwork. The acrid smoke of burning hair and hide lofted around them, and their hands were bloody as they notched the ears and castrated the little bull calves with their thin-bladed knives. It was hard scab-handed work and dangerous if you were new to it, or just awkward and given to daydreaming.

I was all those things, so I was among the three or four who were left with the tiresome job we called "holding cows." We were stationed around the perimeter of the little herd, just keeping the cows and their calves together in a milling way until the ropers had done their work, and Dollarhide shouted, and another branding was finished. What we mostly did was sit quietly beyond the fringes of the herd on whatever horse it was that day and wait to ride on and gather and brand another 70 or 100 calves before heading back in the late afternoon to the wagon, which was camped at Rock Spring or South Corral or one of those places. We traveled at the long, jolting, killer pace Dollarhide preferred, all of us strung-out behind, across the sage flats in going to our second and last meal of the day, hoping maybe the cook had opened a few cans of chilled tomatoes to go with the fried steak and milk gravy and chopped spuds and biscuits. Canned tomatoes were our fruit dish on that desert, where a drink of the springwater was a luxury and pancake syrup mixed with butter was candy.

Maybe I was dreaming of some such thing when Dollarhide, right before me, got himself in quick and unimaginable trouble. He was riding a long-legged black with three white stockings and not much in the way of brains, a big four-year-old one of the young bucks had broken to the bridle that spring. The horse was just learning the rudiments of calf roping. There had been a lot of brainless skittering and crow-hopping around, but nothing serious while the old man roped and dragged a couple of small calves. But then he swung a big loop and caught a yearling bull calf that had been missed by this same branding crew the previous fall. He caught that bull calf right around the middle, very bad form, and the rodeo started.

The yearling weighed close to 500 pounds, all quick bullish energy, and he ducked himself sideways and backwards just as Dollarhide dropped the loop at him—one of those things that happened every so often in a chancy world—and there you had the situation. The yearling bull calf was caught securely around the belly and not by the hind feet at all, surprising the old man, who had maybe been paying more attention to his knot-headed horse than to his roping. The yearling cut back in a wide swing, and Dollarhide, already cursing as he spurred that long-legged horse, was trying to get its head around to face the rope.

The rest of it was slow motion. The rawhide riata came cutting up under the black horse's tail, goosing the horse who went straight up and came down into a twisting bucking exhibition that would have looked fine in Champion of the World competitions. Dollarhide had seen what was coming and already had turned loose his turns of rope on the saddle horn to getting clear rid of the riata, but he was half-way unseated by surprise. They were out in the rocks and brush, and the stocking-footed gelding plunged and nearly fell before going high in another twisting leap. It looked as though the old man might come down hard, and this was no joke, not for anybody, out in those lava-rocks. A young man might escape with bad bruises and cuts, but a man of sixty might likely break in two or three places.

Then I saw it: the old man got hold of the saddle horn with both hands, and he pulled leather, and he stayed up there, out of his stirrups and everywhere on that gone-crazy horse. But Dollarhide stayed up there and not down, pulling leather like any greenhorn on that day when we were branding calves on the Gooch Plateau. He made the ride, nothing clean and pretty about it, with his head snapping and his hat gone. Those lava boulders with their etchings of lichen were all around him if he should come loose. Our legendary rider pulled leather until the gelding wore down, and then Dollarhide was back in the saddle, and the show was over.

The old man spurred the gelding and came trotting back to us, the both of them breathless. A little whirlwind of craziness had gone by, leaving nothing much damaged but my belief in legends. Dollarhide got down off the gelding, rolled a cigarette, put his hat back on his head, and caught me staring. "Boy," he said, "this ain't a time to get killed. Not for wages."

⌀

We grew up and dreamed of rodeos and those tight-bodied little buckle-chasing bunnies, with high-crowned white hats tipped back and wide purple ribbons trailing down to their asses, who used to hang around behind the bucking chutes. You know, the horn blows, the ride has been nothing but a rocking chair, and you kick loose and land running and then limp your way back to the chutes while the crowd goes on cheering. And there she is. Perfect teeth. Dreaming her own kind of dreams.

We had a lot of those fantasies, late evenings around the cook fire after a back-breaking day in the scab-rock country between South Corral and Sagehen Spring, where I served my horseback apprenticeship. "They're gonna put me in the movies, they're gonna make a big star out of me."

Or not. We always suspected, as part of our suspicion of anything citified, that any dream of rodeo always had at its center a sinkhole spiraling down toward night-town, drunk-man darkness, and brain damage of the most devastating kind. Or lost and pointless death, the kind that always happens to somebody else, like asphyxiation in the backseat of a secondhand car while it idles in a wintertime drive-in movie south of Bakersfield, California. That happened to somebody I knew.

Even glory had its dark-side-of-the-moon aspects. In 1980, in the IL chuck-wagon tent, sipping coffee and eating fresh-baked apple pie, Tom Anderson and I talked of Dollarhide and his son, Rossie, who is dead, too, and the night Rossie fought Beef Miller outside Hunters Lodge in Lakeview, and we wondered what had become of Tootie Gunderson, who was tending bar that long-ago night. Last either of us knew she was running a bar down in Cottonwood, California. Since then, after she read this, she called from Oklahoma.

The fight with Beef Miller had to do with Rossie having been Champion of the World at bulldogging in 1953, with the huge silver buckle on his belt, and with him being white and Beef being Indian and the essential crookedness—racist and otherwise—of rodeo judging, and all the other resentments inherent therein. It wasn't any joke, and it isn't in hindsight. Two large men and they beat each other bloody. I watched, and the next day I was sick drunk in the hayfield.

I only saw Rossie Dollarhide one more time. Imagine way off to the west there is a Technicolor glow to the sunset scheme of things over Warner Valley, pink shadows and in the sky a crossing of feathery disintegrating jet-stream contrails. I had lately watched the first Beatles concert on our only channel of television and sensed that uncanny things were beginning out in the Great World. I was not taking part. I was stranded in the deep West and because of that felt my life was lost.

This particular evening I was irrigating, which is a different process than may immediately come to mind, an art we called "balancing water," adjusting headgates and running pumps along our hundred or so miles of interwoven canal system to make sure nothing flooded before morning. None of that mucking around with a #2 shovel, no hip boots; but ramming along levee banks in a 1961 Ford pickup at 50 miles an hour, balancing water and attempting to balance my country life against desire. Barley was coming up in long even rows against the sunset light and timothy in the meadows, waterbirds were going north to their summer life on the tundra, my children were with their horses, my wife was in our home, and so much more. I weighed all this against the burning news that I wanted to be somewhere else, nearby to that mysterious frenzy of energy echoing from the grainy images of the Beatles and their manic hordes. I wanted their high times. I wanted to be *somebody*.

Along comes trouble. Across the middle of our valley, a couple of years before, the state had built a highway. After I parked and opened the wire gate into the Big Beef Field, I heard the soft humming of an oncoming automobile traveling toward me with all the speed built up on that 100-mile-an-hour voyage across the deserts of northern Nevada. With the gate open, I stood and watched it come at me out of the twilight.

It was a pink Cadillac convertible of the tail-fin era, running without headlights. It began to slow and ended up coasting to a halt on the highway alongside where I stood. The top was down, and the dark bareheaded man riding shotgun was Rossie Dollarhide, who by that time was living mostly in Los Angeles, on the fringes of the movie business, near the heart of mythology. The driver was another rodeo cowboy whose name I forget, a compact little blond fellow who never said anything but, "Damn straight." Otherwise, the cat had got his tongue.

Rossie was another matter, a huge and agile man who by that time had broken one of his legs so many times, had even ridden with it broken, that he was forced to wear a steel brace strapped on outside his Levis. That brace was like an emblem of courage and heedlessness.

Rossie handed me a warm quart of Miller's and climbed out to stand beside me in the twilight. He wanted to talk. Maybe five years older than me, he was an authentic rodeo hero. When I was a kid working summers around the desert chuck wagon, he was riding the rough string. So we knew each other, in the way little kids know the school-yard big kids. And now here I was, working like a farmer for wages, and there he was, a former Champion of the World sporting that emblematic steel brace and wearing his silver-and-gold Champion of the World buckle as he traveled in a pink Cadillac with no front windshield. The windshield was not broken out, but missing entirely, as if it had never been there.

"Looks like a windy sonofabitch," I said.

"Damn straight," said the driver, studying the road ahead.

Rossie paid us no attention. "This is not pretty," he said. "Would you take a look at this?" He leaned close, and the odor of lemon shaving lotion was fairly overwhelming.

"What's that?" I said.

"Bugs. I got bugs plastered all over my face."

Thinking back about Rossie and the bugs, I am reminded of Gregory Peck in *The Gunfighter* as he sat under a clock in the glow of his barroom-gunfighter fame and waited as destiny galloped closer, knowing well that in the real West it was horsemanship and not skill with a six-gun that defined a man. Knowing he had gone wrong.

"Thirty-four years old," Gregory Peck said, "and I never even owned a decent watch." He was seriously saddened by the fact, as Ross was by the mosquitoes.

The conversation never got beyond that, but I knew what Rossie was telling me. He felt trapped by a foolish sport he had mistaken for a purpose. As I felt trapped in agriculture. They drove away, and I went on balancing my water, the warm quart of Miller's between my knees as I drove, dumb with yearning to be along for the ride on that wandering adventure, if that's what it was. From the vantage of these years later I see that Rossie and I were mourning the demise of an older sense of what was proper, in which I would not have envied his venturesome skills, and he would not have looked at my foot-soldier life as anything he needed.

We were grieving for the world of his father and my grandfather. Although the elder Dollarhide, the old man, never owned an acre of ground anywhere I knew about, and my grandfather made a concerted effort to own them all, they were equal men before the world in a real and quite unromantic way. Property, in that old world, did not make the man, but what did was rather something about being centered in life, what was happening right at the moment. To understand, all you had to do was watch Old Man

Dollarhide cutting dry cows from the cows and calves in the fall of the year on a quick little bay horse named Tinkertoy. The old man never suspected the importance of anything beyond what he was doing, or at least he never let on. It was the loss of such undivided minds and lives and nostalgia for work that mattered and a range-land sense of proportion—it was getting at us both; the loss of direct knowledge of what to do next and who we were supposed to be.

Rossie died around Flagstaff, Arizona; he was killed while working as a movie extra. His horse fell, and he took a rib through a lung. Apparently he just roughed it out in that old cowboy way and didn't say anything about needing a medical man and went back to his motel and drowned in his blood some time in the night while trying to sleep. The story goes like that. Confusion and things carried too far.

We used to talk about those silver-and-gold buckles with your name engraved under magic words that would turn all the rest of your life just the slightest degree anticlimactic: *Champion of the World.* We used to guess at how much they would weigh, what they would feel like on your belt.

An existence thick with dreams. In 1980, the young boys branding there that morning on the IL Ranch were like ghosts of what I most seriously wanted for a long time in my life. While they were roping and dragging calves, I cooked a half-dozen nuts—mountain oysters, testicles, whatever you know them by—on that juniper fire, right there nestling on the glowing charcoal. As I chewed them I got centered back into what I had once been. I found myself understanding what I had gone away hunting for and why coming back here was not a sappy sentiment-filled thing to do.

In the summer of 1945 I was 13 and the buckaroo crew was haying the IXL, a ranch my grandfather leased from the Charles Sheldon Antelope Refuge in Nevada, south of the Oregon border in Guano Valley. The haying took maybe three weeks and kept the crew busy during a slack season. At least nobody had gone to tractors yet.

There were ten or twelve of us, counting the kids, me and my cousin and another wrango boy. As much as anything, this story is about the wrango boy, who herded the horses and hauled firewood and water for the cook, and peeled potatoes. Because that wrango boy, more than any of us, I think, had his eye on the Great World. All that month we were riding bucking horses after supper and most of the day on Sundays. Somebody had their rodeo bucking string running in the hills back of the IXL. We built a bucking chute in a stout round corral, and the fun was on.

God, did I hate it. One thing I would never claim is any ability on horseback. Every Sunday I would get pitched into the fence or onto my head about three times. But this wrango boy was different. He rode those bucking horses as if they were a natural easy chair, and I've got no doubt that rodeo looked to him like a getaway route. From what, I don't know.

But right then, in August of 1945, for that crew of men isolated way out there on the highland desert, VJ Day must have looked like another kind of escape. Maybe just from the daily passage of commonplace life. An excuse for fun. Maybe from guilt at having taken an agricultural deferment from the army, thus avoiding the fighting. Those were grave matters.

Anyway, all of them, nine or ten men in Old Man Dollarhide's black V-8 Ford, headed off on the 85 dusty miles to Denio and the nearest barroom. They came back the next morning with cases of whiskey and beer, and soon we were all drunk, even the chuck-wagon cook, an old man named Jack Frost. It was my first time, and I stayed drunk for two days.

About noon it was decided we should move camp to the Doherty Place, an old starved-out homesteader ranch up in the middle of Guano Valley, just off from where the Winnemucca highway passes now. The men took the wagon, and we kids moved the horse herd at a long hard run for around twelve miles. For some reason there were no tragedies. I remember playing hand grenade with canned corn and dropping sacks of flour from the second-story windows at the Doherty Place like high-level bombers, watching them burst on the backs of horses. Finally we threw all the food into the open well, and the men left again in the Ford.

The next morning we were alone, three kids and the old cook, who was howling drunk in his bed, stinking of urine, and could not get up. We managed to harness the teams and load the wagon, including old soggy Jack, who was still in his bed and muttering about dying, and headed for the MC Ranch headquarters, fifty miles across rutted desert roads to Warner Valley.

My cousin and I pulled chicken-shit rank. Because our grandfather owned them, we took the horses and left the wrango boy with the wagon. By late afternoon we were turning the saddle horses loose on the meadows near the ranch house. The wrango boy was two days getting there with the chuck wagon and that poor old cook, in his bed all the time lamenting and threatening to die. A little later, in Lakeview for the Labor Day Rodeo, the last time I ever saw him, that boy looked at me with hot eyes and said, "That's it for you sons-a-bitches."

We were in one of those old double-duty barbershops, which are gone from the country now, where a man in off the desert could get himself shaved and have his hair cut and then take himself an opulent two-hour bath where all the hot water you wanted was $1.50. Then get into fresh clothes from the skin out and be ready for town. That former wrango boy stood there looking at me with his hair combed down and wet, wearing a new yellow shirt bought around the corner at the Lakeview Mercantile, and all at once he was a grown-up and I wasn't. He just shook his head and turned away.

What he was telling me was simple. At maybe fifteen, he was confirmed into an intention of never again being wrango boy for anybody, not ever. When my chance came, I got away from the ranch, too, looking for a way to be someone else, someone who was not the owner's kid—and that slick-faced youngster with his yellow shirt and his hair wetted down, glaring at me, got away to go rodeoing and was mildly famous for a while. Right then in America, at least in Lake County, the high desert country of Oregon, what all of us wanted was escape and connection with the Great World.

At the Doherty Place in Guano Valley, where we threw the food down the well that afternoon in 1945, there was a raggedy pale oilcloth tacked to the bullpen walls. On it were written lists of names. Ross Dollarhide, Earnest Messner, Casper Gunderson, Hugh Cahill, Cliff Gunderson. The lists began back before World War II: the names of men who rode for the MC. But about twenty years ago some archivist or thief tore down that oilcloth from those walls and took it and those lists away. To preserve, I hope, somewhere.

Heroes are defined as individuals who go out into the world, leaving home on a quest. They endure trials of initiation and return changed, seeing the world in a fresh way, bearing the wisdom of their experience as news that serves the stay-at-homes in their efforts toward making sense of themselves and of what they are attempting to make of their lives.

Some of us dreamed of going away to such heroism.

And now it looks as if things have changed. People are staying home, in that part of the country where they know how
to live and what to care about. In some large blurry sense,
there no longer seems to be too much currency in the idea
that going away to seek your fortune is any sensible road
toward anything that matters. Nobody imagines that either
the Beatles or big-time rodeo will save your life.

Life on the high desert looks better than it did in the old
days. Maybe the wages are not much, but the food is fine.
In my childhood, canned tomatoes all around was a big
deal. At the IL wagon, the noontime I was there, they were
finishing up with apple-and-raisin pie about three inches
deep. An old-timer named Harold Smith was eating it with
sweet canned milk. In that life you learn to wait for simple,
specific pleasures.

After scraping their plates, they all went out to the
rope corral and climbed up aboard their afternoon horses,
which had been caught in a ceremony that's ancient among
horseback people—one man, the boss, in the center with a
riata catching horses with names like Snowball and Snuffy
while each rider chose his from the string. The white called
Snowball crow-hopped a little before he settled down. Then
they rode away to another sweep across the sagebrush desert, another branding that afternoon, riding unhurriedly
into another horseback turn of life.

Owning It All

I N THE SLOW HISTORY of our country in the far reaches
of southeastern Oregon, a backlands enclave even in the
American West, the first settlers arrived a decade after the
end of the Civil War. I've learned to think of myself as having had the luck to grow up at the tail end of a way of exist-
ing in which people lived in everyday proximity to animals
on territory they knew more precisely than the patterns in
the palms of their hands.

In Warner Valley we understood our property as others
know their cities, a landscape of neighborhoods, some sacred,
some demonic, some habitable, some not, which is as the sea,
they tell me, is understood by fishermen. It was only later, in
college, that I learned it was possible to understand Warner
as a fertile oasis in a vast featureless sagebrush desert.

Over in that other world on the edge of rain forests that
is the Willamette Valley of Oregon, I'd gone to school in
General Agriculture, absorbed in a double-bind sort of learning, studying to center myself in the County Agent/Corps
of Engineers mentality they taught and at the same time
taking classes from Bernard Malamud and wondering with
great romantic fervor if it was in me to write the true history of the place where I had always lived.

Straight from college I went to Photo Intelligence work
in the Air Force. The last couple of those years were spent

deep in the jungle on the island of Guam, where we lived in a little compound of cleared land, in a Quonset hut.

The years on Guam were basically happy and bookish: we were newly married, with children. A hundred or so yards north of our Quonset hut, along a trail through the luxuriant undergrowth between coconut palms and banana trees, a ragged cliff of red porous volcanic rock fell directly to the ocean. When the Pacific typhoons came roaring in, our hut was washed with blowing spray from the great breakers. On calm days we would stand on the cliff at that absolute edge of our jungle and island and gaze out across to the island of Rota, and to the endlessness of ocean beyond, and I would marvel at my life, so far from southeastern Oregon.

And then in the late fall of 1958, after I had been gone from Warner Valley for eight years, I came back to participate in our agriculture. The road in had been paved, we had Bonneville Power on lines from the Columbia River, and high atop the western rim of the valley there was a TV translator, which beamed fluttering pictures from New York and Los Angeles direct to us.

And I had changed, or thought I had, for a while. No more daydreams about writing the true history. Try to understand my excitement as I climbed to the rim behind our house and stood there by our community TV translator. The valley where I had always seen myself living was open before me like another map and playground, and this time I was an adult, and high up in the War Department. Looking down maybe 3,000 feet into Warner, and across to the high basin and range desert where we summered our cattle, I saw the beginnings of my real life as an agricultural manager. The flow of watercourses in the valley was spread before me like a map, and I saw it as a surgeon might see the flow of blood across a chart of anatomy, and saw myself helping to turn the fertile home place of my childhood into a machine for agriculture whose features could be delineated with the same surgeon's precision in my mind.

It was work that can be thought of as craftsmanlike, both artistic and mechanical, creating order according to an ideal of beauty based on efficiency, manipulating the forces of water and soil, season and seed, manpower and equipment, laying out functional patterns for irrigation and cultivation on the surface of our valley. We drained and leveled, ditched and pumped, and for a long while our crops were all any of us could have asked. There were over 5,000 water control devices. We constructed a perfect agricultural place, and it was sacred, so it seemed.

Agriculture is often envisioned as an art, and it can be. Of course there is always survival, and bank notes, and all that. But your basic bottom line on the farm is again and again some notion of how life should be lived. The majority of agricultural people, if you press them hard enough, even though most of them despise sentimental abstractions, will admit they are trying to create a good place, and to live as part of that goodness, in the kind of connection that with fine reason we call *rootedness*. It's just that there is good art and bad art.

These are thoughts that come back when I visit eastern Oregon. I park and stand looking down into the lava-rock and juniper-tree canyon where Deep Creek cuts its way out of the Warner Mountains, and the great turkey buzzard soars high in the yellow-orange light above the evening. The fishing water is low, as it always is in late August, unfurling itself around dark and broken boulders. The trout, I know, are hanging where the currents swirl across themselves, waiting for the one entirely precise and lucky cast, the Renegade fly bobbing toward them.

Even now I can see it, each turn of water along miles of that creek. Walk some stretch enough times with a fly rod and its configurations will imprint themselves on your being with Newtonian exactitude. Which is beyond doubt one of the attractions of such fishing—the hours of learning, and then the intimacy with a living system that carries you beyond the sadness of mere gaming for sport.

What I liked to do, back in the old days, was pack in some spuds and an onion and corn flour and spices mixed up in a plastic bag, a small cast-iron frying pan in my wicker creel and, in the late twilight on a gravel bar by the water, cook up a couple of rainbows over a fire of snapping dead willow and sage, eating alone while the birds flitted through the last hatch, wiping my greasy fingers on my pants while the heavy trout began rolling at the lower ends of the pools.

The canyon would be shadowed under the moon when I walked out to show up home empty-handed, to sit with my wife over a drink of whiskey at the kitchen table. Those nights I would go to bed and sleep without dreams, a grown-up man secure in the house and the western valley where he had been a child, enclosed in a topography of spirit he assumed he knew more closely than his own features in the shaving mirror.

So, I ask myself, if it was such a pretty life, why didn't I stay? The peat soil in Warner Valley was deep and rich, we ran good cattle, and my most sacred memories are centered there. What could run me off?

Well, for openers, it got harder and harder to get out of bed in the mornings and face the days, for reasons I didn't understand. More and more I sought the comfort of fishing that knowable creek. Or in winter the blindness of television.

My father grew up on a homestead place on the sagebrush flats outside Silver Lake, Oregon. He tells of hiding under the bed with his sisters when strangers came to the gate. He grew up, as we all did in that country and era, believing that the one sure defense against the world was property. I was born in 1932 and recall a life before the end of World War II in which it was possible for a child to imagine that his family owned the world.

Warner Valley was largely swampland when my grandfather bought the MC Ranch with no down payment in 1936, right at the heart of the Great Depression. The outside work was done mostly by men and horses and mules, and our ranch valley was filled with life. In 1937 my father bought his first track-layer, a secondhand RD6 Caterpillar he used to build a 17-mile diversion canal to carry the spring floodwater around the east side of the valley, and we were on our way to draining all swamps. The next year he bought an RD7 and a John Deere 36 combine that cut an 18-foot swath, and we were deeper into the dream of power over nature and men, which I had begun to inhabit while playing those long-ago games of war.

The peat ground left by the decaying remnants of ancient tule beds was diked into huge undulating grain fields— Houston Swamp with 750 irrigated acres, Dodson Lake with 800—a final total of almost 8,000 acres under cultivation, and for reasons of what seemed like common sense and efficiency, the work became industrialized. Our artistry worked toward a model whose central image was the machine.

The natural patterns of drainage were squared into dragline ditches, the tules and the aftermath of the oat and barley crops were burned—along with a little more of the combustible peat soil every year. We flood-irrigated when the water came in spring, drained in late March, and planted in a 24-hour-a-day frenzy that began around April 25 and ended—with luck—by the 10th of May, just as leaves on the Lombardy poplar were breaking from their buds. We

summered our cattle on more than a million acres of Taylor
Grazing Land across the high lava-rock and sagebrush desert out east of the valley, miles of territory where we owned
most of what water there was, and it was ours. We owned
it all, or so we felt. The government was as distant as news
on the radio.

The most intricate part of my job was called "balancing
water," a night and day process of opening and closing pipes
and redwood headgates and running the 18-inch drainage
pumps. That system was the finest plaything I ever had.

And despite the mud and endless hours, the work remained play for a long time, the making of a thing both functional and elegant. We were doing God's labor and creating
a good place on earth, living the pastoral yeoman dream—
that's how our mythology defined it, although nobody would
ever have thought to talk about work in that way.

And then it all went dead, over years, but swiftly.

You can imagine our surprise and despair, our sense of
having been profoundly cheated. It took us a long while
to realize some unnameable thing was wrong, and then we
blamed it on ourselves, our inability to manage enough. But
the fault wasn't ours, beyond the fact that we had all been
educated to believe in a grand bad factory-land notion as
our prime model of excellence.

We felt enormously betrayed. For so many years, through
endless efforts, we had proceeded in good faith, and it turned
out we had wrecked all we had not left untouched. The beloved migratory rafts of waterbirds, the green-headed mallards and the redheads and canvasbacks, the cinnamon teal
and the great Canadian honkers, were mostly gone along
with their swampland habitat. The hunting, in so many
ways, was no longer what it had been.

We wanted to build a reservoir, and litigation started.
Our laws were being used against us, by people who wanted

a share of what we thought of as our water. We could not endure the boredom of our mechanical work and couldn't hire anyone who cared enough to do it right. We baited the coyotes with 1080, and rodents destroyed our alfalfa; we sprayed weeds and insects with 2-4-D Ethyl and Mala-thion, and Parathion for clover mite, and we shortened our own lives.

In quite an actual way we had come to victory in the artistry of our playground warfare against all that was natu-rally alive in our native home. We had reinvented our valley according to the most persuasive ideal given us by our cul-ture, and we ended with a landscape organized like a ma-chine for growing crops and fattening cattle, a machine that creaked a little louder each year, a dreamland gone wrong.

One of my strongest memories comes from a morning when I was maybe ten years old, out on the lawn before our country home in spring, beneath a bluebird sky. I was watching the waterbirds coming off the valley swamps and grain fields where they had been feeding overnight. They were going north to nesting grounds on the Canadian tun-dra, and that piece of morning, inhabited by the sounds of their wings and their calling in the clean air, was wonder-filled and magical. I was enclosed in a living place.

No doubt that memory has persisted because it was a sight of possibility that I will always cherish—an image of the great good place rubbed smooth over the years like a river stone, which I touch again as I consider why life in Warner Valley went so seriously haywire. But never again in my lifetime will it be possible for a child to stand out on a bright spring morning in Warner Valley and watch the waterbirds come through in enormous, rafting vee-shaped flocks of thousands—and I grieve.

A couple of decades ago my father and I were driving up the Bitterroot Valley of Montana, and he was gazing away to the mountains. "They'll never see it the way we did," he said, and I wonder what he saw.

We shaped our piece of the West according to the model provided by our mythology, and instead of a great good place such order had given us enormous power over nature and a blank perfection of fields.

A mythology can be understood as a story that contains a set of implicit instructions from a society to its members, telling them what is valuable and how to conduct themselves if they are to preserve the things they cherish.

The teaching mythology we grew up with in the American West is a pastoral story of agricultural ownership. The story begins with a vast innocent continent, natural and almost magically alive, capable of inspiring us to reverence and awe, and yet savage, a wilderness. A good rural people come from the East, and they take the land from its native inhabitants, and tame it for agricultural purposes, bringing civilization: a notion of how to live embodied in law. The story is as old as invading armies, and at heart it is a racist, sexist, imperialist mythology of conquest; a rationale for violence—against other people and against nature.

At the same time, that mythology is a lens through which we continue to see ourselves. Many of us like to imagine ourselves as honest yeomen who sweat and work in the woods or the mines or the fields for a living. And many of us are. We live in a real family, a work-centered society, and we like to see ourselves as people with the good luck and sense to live in a place where some vestige of the natural world still exists in working order. Many of us hold that natural world as sacred to some degree, just as it is in our myth. Lately, more and more of us are coming to understand our society in the American West as an exploited colony, threatened by greedy outsiders who want to take our sacred place away from us, or at least to strip and degrade it.

In short, we see ourselves as a society of mostly decent people who live with some connection to a holy wilderness, threatened by those who lust for power and property. We look for Shane to come riding out of the Tetons, and instead we see Exxon and the Sierra Club. One looks virtually as alien as the other.

And our mythology tells us we own the West, absolutely and morally—we own it because of our history. Our people brought law to this difficult place, they suffered and they shed blood and they survived, and they earned this land for us. Our efforts have surely earned us the right to absolute control over the thing we created. The myth tells us this place is ours, and will always be ours, to do with as we see fit.

That's a most troubling and enduring message because we want to believe it, and we do believe it, so many of us, despite its implicit ironies and wrongheadedness, despite the fact that we took the land from someone else. We try to ignore a genocidal history of violence against the Native Americans.

In the American West we are struggling to revise our dominant mythology and to find a new story to inhabit. Laws control our lives, and they are designed to preserve a model of society based on values learned from mythology. Only after reimagining our myths can we coherently remodel our laws and hope to keep our society in a realistic relationship to what is actual.

In Warner Valley we thought we were living the right lives, creating a great precise perfection of fields, and we found the mythology had been telling us an enormous lie. The world had proven too complex, or the myth too simple-minded. And we were mortally angered.

The truth is, we never owned all the land and water. We

don't even own very much of them, privately. And we don't own anything absolutely or forever. As our society grows more and more complex and interwoven, our entitlement becomes less and less absolute, more and more likely to be legally diminished. Our rights to property will never take precedence over the needs of society. Nor should they, we all must agree in our grudging hearts. Ownership of property has always been a privilege granted by society, and revokable.

☙

Down by the slaughterhouse my grandfather used to keep a chicken-wire cage for trapping magpies. The cage was as high as a man's head and mounted on a sled so it could be towed off and cleaned. It worked on the same principle as a lobster trap. Those iridescent black-and-white birds could get in to feed on the intestines of butchered cows—we never butchered a fat heifer or steer for our own consumption, only aged dry cows culled from the breeding herd— but they couldn't get out.

Trapped under the noontime sun, the magpies would flutter around in futile exploration for a while and then would give in to a great sullen presentiment of their fate, just hopping around and picking at leftovers and waiting.

My grandfather was Scots-English and a very old man by then, but his blue eyes never turned watery and lost. He was one of those cowmen we don't see so often anymore, heedless of most everything outside his playground, which was livestock and seasons and property, and, as the seasons turned, more livestock and more property, a game that could be called accumulation.

All the notes were paid off, and you would have thought my grandfather would have been secure and released to ease back in wisdom.

But no such luck. It seemed he had to keep proving his ownership. This took various forms, like endless litigation, which I have heard described as the sport of kings, but the manifestation I recall most vividly was that of killing magpies.

In the summer the ranch hands would butcher in the after-supper cool of an evening a couple of times a week. About once a week, when a number of magpies had gathered in the trap, maybe 10 or 15, my grandfather would get out his lifetime 12-gauge shotgun and have someone drive him down to the slaughterhouse in his dusty, ancient gray Cadillac, so he could look over his catch and get down to the business at hand. Once there, the ritual was slow and dignified, and always inevitable as one shoe after another.

The old man would sit there awhile in his Cadillac and gaze at the magpies with his merciless blue eyes, and the birds would stare back with their hard black eyes. The summer dust would settle around the Cadillac, and the silent confrontation would continue. It would last several minutes.

Then my grandfather would sigh, swing open the door on his side of the Cadillac, and climb out, dragging his shotgun behind him, the pockets of his gray gabardine suit-coat like a frayed uniform bulging with shells. The stock of the shotgun had been broken sometime deep in the past, and it was wrapped with fine brass wire, which shone golden in the sunlight while the old man thumbed shells into the magazine. All this without saying a word.

In the ear of my mind I try to imagine the radio playing softly in the Cadillac, something like "Room Full of Roses" or "Candy Kisses," but there was no radio. There was just the ongoing hum of insects and the clacking of the mechanism as the old man pumped a shell into the firing chamber.

He would lift the shotgun, and from no more than twelve feet, sighting down that barrel where the bluing was mostly worn off, through the chicken wire into the eyes of those trapped magpies, he would kill them one by one, taking his time, maybe so as to prove that this was no accident.

He would fire and there would be a minor explosion of blood and feathers, the huge booming of the shotgun echoing through the flattening light of early afternoon, off the sage-covered hills and down across the hay meadows and the sloughs lined with dagger-leafed willow, frightening great flights of blackbirds from fence lines nearby, to rise in flocks and wheel and be gone.

"Bastards," my grandfather would mutter, and then he would take his time about killing another, and finally he would be finished and turn without looking back, and climb into his side of the Cadillac, where the door still stood open. Whoever's turn it was that day would drive him back up the willow-lined lane through the meadows to the ranch house beneath the Lombardy poplar, to the cool shaded living room with its faded linoleum where the old man would finish out his day playing pinochle with my grandmother and anyone else he could gather, sometimes taking a break to retune a favorite program on the Zenith Trans-Oceanic radio.

No one in our family, so far as I ever heard, knew any reason why the old man had come to hate magpies with such specific intensity in his old age. The blackbirds were endlessly worse, the way they would mass together in flocks of literally thousands, to strip and thrash in his oat and barley fields, and then feed all fall in the bins of grain stockpiled to fatten his cattle.

"Where is the difference?" I asked him once, about the magpies.

"Because they're mine," he said. I never did know exactly what he was talking about, the remnants of entrails left over from the butchering of culled stocker cows, or the magpies. But it became clear he was asserting his absolute lordship over both, and over me, too, so long as I was living on his property. For all his life and most of mine the notion of property as absolute seemed like law, even when it never was.

Most of us who grew up owning land in the West believed that any impairment of our right to absolute control of that property was a taking, forbidden by the so-called "taking clause" of the Constitution. We believed regulation of our property rights could never legally reduce the value of our property. After all, what was the point of ownership if it was not profitable? Any infringement on the control of private property was a Communist perversion.

But all over the West, as in all of America, the old folkway of property as an absolute right is dying. Our mythology doesn't work anymore.

We find ourselves weathering a rough winter of discontent, snared in the uncertainties of a transitional time and urgently yearning to inhabit a story that might bring sensible order to our lives—even as we know such a story can only evolve through an almost literally infinite series of recognitions of what, individually, we hold sacred. The liberties our people came seeking are more and more constrained, and here in the West, as everywhere, we hate it.

Simple as that. And we have to live with it. There is no more running away to territory. This is it, for most of us. We have no choice but to live in community. If we're lucky we may discover a story that teaches us to abhor our old romance with conquest and possession.

My grandfather died in 1958, toppling out of his chair at the pinochle table, soon after I came back to Warner, but his vision dominated our lives until we sold the ranch in 1967. An ideal of absolute ownership that defines family as property is the perfect device for driving people away from one another. There was a rule in our family. "What's good for the property is good for you."

"Every time there was more money we bought land,"
my grandmother proclaimed after learning my grandfather
had been elected to the Cowboy Hall of Fame. I don't know
if she spoke with pride or bitterness, but I do know that,
having learned to understand love as property, we were all
absolutely divided at the end; relieved to escape amid a
litany of divorce and settlements, our family broken in the
getaway.

I cannot grieve for my grandfather. It is hard to imagine,
these days, that any man could ever again think he owns
the birds.

Thank the Lord there were other old men involved in my
upbringing. My grandfather on my mother's side ran away
from a Germanic farmstead in Wisconsin the year he was
fourteen, around 1900, and made his way to Butte. "I was
lucky," he would say. "I was too young to go down in the
mines, so they put me to sharpening steel."

Seems to me such a boy must have been lucky to find
work at all, wandering the teeming difficult streets of the
most urban city in the American West. "Well, no," he said.
"They put you to work. It wasn't like that. They were good
to me in Butte. They taught me a trade. That's all I did was
work. But it didn't hurt me any."

After most of ten years on the hill—broke and on strike,
still a very young man—he rode the rails south to the silver
mines in what he called "Old Mexico," and then worked
his way back north through the mining country of Nevada
in time for the glory days in Goldfield and Rhyolite and
Tonopah. At least those are the stories he would tell. "This
Las Vegas," he would say. "When I was there you could
have bought it all for a hundred and fifty dollars. Cost you
ten cents for a drink of water."

To my everlasting sadness, I never really quizzed him on

the facts. Now I look at old photographs of those mining camps and wonder. It's difficult for me to imagine the good gentle man I knew walking those tough dusty streets. He belonged, at least in those Butte days, to the International Brotherhood of Blacksmiths and Helpers. I still have his first dues card. He was initiated July 11, 1904, and most of the months of 1904 and 1905 are stamped, DUES PAID.

Al died in an old folks' home in Eugene, Oregon. During the days of his last summer, when he knew the jig was up, a fact he seemed to regard with infallible good humor, we would sit in his room and listen to the aged bemused woman across the hall chant her litany of childhood, telling herself that she was somebody and still real.

It was always precisely the same story, word by particular word. I wondered then how much of it was actual, lifting from some deep archive in her memory, and now I wonder how much of it was pure sweet invention, occasioned by the act of storytelling and by the generative, associative power of language. I cannot help but think of ancient fires, light flickering on the faces of children and storytellers detailing the history of their place in the scheme of the earth.

The story itself started with a screen door slamming and her mother yelling at her when she was a child coming out from the back porch of a white house, and rotting apples on the ground under the trees in the orchard, and a dog that snapped at the flies. "Mother," she would exclaim in exasperation, "I'm fine."

The telling took about three minutes, and she told it like a story for grandchildren. "That's nice," she would say to her dog. "That's nice."

Then she would lapse into quiet, rewinding herself, seeing an old time when the world contained solace enough to seem complete, and she would start over again, going on until she had lulled herself back into sleep. I would wonder if she was dreaming about that dog amid the fallen apples, snapping at flies and yellowjackets.

At the end she would call the name of that dog over and over in a quavering, beseeching voice—and my grandfather would look to me from his bed and his eyes would be gleaming with laughter, such an old man laughing painfully, his shoulders shaking, and wheezing.

"Son of a bitch," he would whisper, when she was done calling the dog again, and he would wipe the tears from his face with the sleeve of his hospital gown. *Son of a bitch.* He would look to me again, and other than aimless grinning acknowledgment that some mysterious thing was truly funny, I wouldn't know what to do, and then he would look away to the open window, beyond which a far-off lawn mower droned, like this time he was the one who was embarrassed. Not long after that he was dead, and so was the old woman across the hall.

"Son of a bitch," I thought, when we were burying Al one bright afternoon in Eugene, and I found myself suppressing laughter. Maybe it was just a way of ditching my grief for myself, who did not know him well enough to really understand what he thought was funny. I have Al's picture framed on my wall, and I can still look to him and find relief from the old insistent force of my desire to own things. His laughter is like a gift.

Who Owns the West

After a half-mile in soft rain on the slick hayfield stubble, I would crouch behind the levee and listen to the gentle clatter of the waterbirds talking, and surprise them into flight, maybe a half-dozen mallard hens and three green-headed drakes lifting in silhouetted loveliness against the November twilight, hanging only a dozen yards from the end of my shotgun. This was called jump-shooting, or meat-hunting. It almost always worked. But I wish someone had told me reasons you should not necessarily kill the birds. I wish I'd been told to kill ducks only once or twice a winter, for a fine meal with children and friends, and that nine times out of ten I was going to be happier if I let the goddamned birds fly away.

In 1959 on the MC Ranch, an agricultural property my family owned where the western edge of the Great Basin intersects the Oregon/Nevada border, at twenty-seven, I was prideful with a young man's ambition, at the peak of my energetic powers and just that moment happy as such a creature can be. I was centered in the world of my upbringing, king of my mountain, and certain I was deep into the management of perfection. It was my job to run a ranch-hand cookhouse and supervise the labors of from ten to twenty-five working men. Or, to name it most crudely, as was often done, "hire and fire and work the winos."

Think of it as a skill, learnable as any other. As in any profession there are rules, the most basic being enlightened self-interest. Take care of your men, and they will take care of you. And understand their fragilities because you are the one responsible for taking care. Will they fall sick to death in the bunkhouse, and is there someone you can call to administer mercy if they do? What attention will you give them as they die?

Some thirty-six miles west of our valley, over the Warner Mountains in the small lumbering and ranching town of Lakeview, a working man's hotel functioned as a sort of hiring hall. There was a rule of thumb about the men you would find there. The best of them wore a good pair of boots laced up tight over wool socks, which meant they were looking for a laboring job. The most hapless would be wearing low-cut city shoes, no socks and no laces. They were looking for a place to hide and never to be hired. It was a rule that worked.

On bright afternoons when my people were scrambling to survive in the Great Depression, my mother was young and fresh as she led me on walks along the crumbling small-town streets of Malin, Oregon, in the Klamath Basin just north of the California border. This was before we moved to the MC Ranch; I was three years old and understood the world as concentric circles of diminishing glory centered on the sun of her smile.

Outside our tight circle of complicity was my father, an energetic stranger named Oscar who came home at night and, before he touched anything, even me or my mother, he rolled up his sleeves over his white forearms and scrubbed his hands in the kitchen sink with coarse gray lava soap. Out beyond him were the turkey herders, and beyond them lay the vast agricultural world, on the fringes of the Tule Lake Reclamation District, where they worked.

What the herders did in the turkey business, as it was practiced by my father, was haul slatted chicken-wire crates full of turkeys around on old flatbed trucks. When they got to the backside of some farm property where nobody was likely to notice, they parked and opened the doors on those crates and turned the turkeys out to roam and feed on the grasshoppers. Sometimes they had permission, sometimes my father had paid a fee, and some of the time it was theft—grazing the turkeys for free. Sometimes they got caught, and my father paid the fee then. And once in a while they had to reload the turkeys into their crates and move on while some farmer watched with a shotgun.

My upbringing taught me to consider the barnyard turkey to be a captive and bitter, rapacious creature, whose eyes were dull with the opaque gleam of pure selfishness, without soul. I had never heard of a wild one. (Some part of our alienation, when we are most isolated, is ecological. We are lonely and long to share what we regard as the dignity of wild animals—this is the phantom so many of us pursue as we hunt, complicating the actual killing into such a double-bind sort of triumph.) The most recent time I had occasion to confront domesticated turkeys up close was in the fall of 1987, while driving red scoria roads in the North Dakota Badlands. We came across farmstead turkeys, and true or not, I took that as a sign we were deep in-country where agriculture meant subsistence. No doubt my horror of turkeys had much to do with my fear of the men who herded them.

From the windows of our single-bedroom apartment on the second floor of the only brick building in Malin, where I slept on a little bed in the living room, we could look south across the rich irrigated potato- and barley-raising country of the Tule Lake Basin and see to California and the lava-field badlands where the Modoc Indians had hidden out from the U.S. Army in the long ago days of their rebellion. I wonder if my mother told me stories of those natives in their caves, and doubt it, but not because she didn't believe in the arts of make-believe.

It's just that my mother would have told me other stories. She grew up loving opera. My grandfather, as I will always understand it even though we were not connected by blood, earned the money for her music lessons as a blacksmith for the California/Oregon Power Company in Klamath Falls. Sharpening steel, as he put it.

So it is unlikely my mother was fond of stories about desperate natives and hold-out killings and the eventual hanging of Captain Jack, the Modoc war chief, at Fort Klamath. That was just the sort of nastiness she was interested in escaping, and besides, we were holding to defensive actions of our own.

After all, my father was reduced to raising turkeys for a living, in a most haphazard fashion. So my mother told me stories about Christmas as perfection realized: candied apples glowing in the light of an intricately decorated tree, and little toy railroads that tooted and circled the room as if the room were the world. And stories about Santa Claus.

But we live in a place more complex than paradise, some would say richer, and I want to tell a story about my terror on Christmas Eve, and the way we were happy anyhow. The trouble began on a bright afternoon with a little skiff of snow on the ground, when my mother took me for my first barbershop haircut, an event that loomed large in our list of preparations for Christmas, and a step into manhood as she defined it.

I was enjoying the notion of such a ceremony and even the snipping of the barber's gentle shears as I sat elevated to manly height by the board across the arms of his chair—

until Santa Claus came in, jerked off his cap and the fringe of snowy hair, and his equally snowy beard, and stood revealed as an unshaven gray-faced man in a Santa Claus suit, who looked as if he could stand a drink from the way his hands were shaking.

The man leered at my kindly barber and muttered something. I suppose he wanted to know how long he would have to wait for a shave. Maybe he had been waiting all day for a barbershop shave. A fine, brave, hangover sort of waiting, all the while entombed in that Santa Claus suit. I screamed. I like to think I was screaming against chaos, in defense of my mother and notions of a proper Christmas and maybe because our Santa Claus, who was not a Santa. With his corded, unshaven neck, he even looked remotely like a turkey as this story turns edgy and nightmarish.

The turkeys had been slaughtered the week before Thanksgiving in a couple of boxcars pulled onto a siding in Tule Lake and were shipped to markets in the East. Everyone was at liberty and making ready to ride out winter on whatever they had managed to accumulate. So the party my parents threw on the night before Christmas had ancient ceremonial resonances. The harvest was done, the turkeys were slaughtered, and the dead season of cold winds was truly begun. It was a time of release into meditation and winter, to await rebirth.

But it was not a children's party. It is difficult to imagine my father at a children's party. As I recall from this distance it was a party for the turkey herders, those men who had helped my father conspire his way through that humiliating summer with those terrible creatures. At least the faces I see in my dream of that yellow kitchen are the faces of those men. Never again, said my mother, and my father agreed, better times were coming, and everybody got drunk.

I had been put down to sleep on the big bed in my parents' bedroom, which was quite a privilege in itself, and it was only late in the night that I woke to a sense of something gone wrong. The sacred place where I lived with my mother had been invaded by loud laughter and hoedown harmonica music and someone stomping and people dancing.

As I stood in the doorway from the bedroom into the kitchen in my little pajamas, nobody saw me for a long moment, until I began my hysterical momma's-boy shrieking. The harmonica playing stopped, and my mother looked shamefaced to me from the middle of the room where she had been dancing with my father while everyone watched. All those faces of people who are mostly dead turned to me, and it was as if I had gotten up and come out of my parents' bedroom into the actuality of a leering nightmare of vivid light and whiskey bottles on the table and those faces glazed with grotesque intentions.

Someone saved it, one of the men, maybe my father, by picking me up and ignoring my wailing as the harmonica music started again, and then I was in my mother's arms as she danced, whirling around the kitchen table and the center of all attention in a world where everything was possible and good while the turkey herders watched and smiled and thought their private thoughts, and it was Christmas at last, in my mother's arms as I have understood it ever since. It was in some ways an initiation to be regretted.

For years the faces of the turkey herders in their otherness, in that bright kitchen, were part of dreams I dreaded as I tried to go to sleep. In struggling against the otherness of the turkey herders I made a start toward indifference to the disenfranchised. I was learning to inhabit distance, from myself and people I should have cared for.

A couple of years later my family moved the hundred miles east to the MC Ranch. My grandfather got the place with

no money down when he was sixty-two years old by pledg-
ing everything he had worked for all his life; he was unable
to resist owning such a kingdom. The move represented an
enormous change in our fortunes.

Warner Valley is that place which is sacred to me as the
main staging ground for my imagination. I see it as an inhabited landscape where the names of people remind me of
places, and the places remind me of what happened there—
a thicket of stories to catch the mind if it might be falling.

It was during the Second World War that wildlife biolo-
gists from up at the college in Corvallis told my father the
sandhill cranes migrating through Warner were rare and
vanishing creatures, to be cherished with the same intensity
as the ring-necked Manchurian pheasants that had been
imported from the hinterlands of China. The nests of sandhill cranes, with their large off-white speckled eggs, were to
be regarded as absolutely precious. "No matter what," my
father said, "you don't break those eggs."

My father was talking to a tall gray-faced man named
Clyde Bolton, who was stuck with a day of riding a drag
made of heavy timbers across winter-feed grounds on the
native meadows of the Thompson Field. Clyde was breaking up cow shit before the irrigating started, so the chips
wouldn't plug in the sickle bars of the John Deere mowing
machines come summer and haying. Clyde was considered
a pensioner since he had a damaged heart that kept him
from heavy work, and he was married to Ada Bolton, the
indispensable woman who cooked and kept house for us.
Clyde milked the three or four cows my father kept and
tended the chickens and the house garden and took naps
in the afternoon. He hadn't hired out for fieldwork, and he
was unhappy. But help was scarce during those years when
so many of the able-bodied were gone to the war, and there
he was, take it or leave it. And he had no real complaint.

Riding that drag wouldn't hurt even a man with a damaged heart. Clyde was a little spoiled. That's what we used to say. Go easy on the hired help long enough, and they will sour on you. A man, we would say, needs to get out in the open air and sweat and blow off the stink.

This was a Saturday morning in April after the frost had gone out, and I was a boy learning the methodologies of fieldwork. The nests my father talked about were hidden down along unmowed margins in the yellow remnants of knee-high meadow grass from the summer before along the willow-lined sloughs through the home fields. "The ones the coons don't get," my father said.

I can see my father's gray-eyed good humor and his fedora stockman's hat pushed back on his forehead as he studied Clyde; I can hear the ironic rasp in his voice. At that time my father was more than ten years younger than I am now, a man recently come to the center of his world. And I can see Clyde Bolton hitching his suspenders and snorting over the idea of keeping an eye out for the nest of some sandhill crane. I can see his disdain.

This going out with Clyde was as close to any formal initiation as I ever got on the ranch. There really wasn't much of anything for me to do, but it was important I get used to the idea of working on days when I was not in school. It wouldn't hurt a damned bit. A boy should learn to help out where he can, and I knew it, so I was struggling to harness the old team of matched bay geldings, Dick and Dan, and my father and Clyde were not offering to help because a boy would never make a man if you helped him all the time.

"You see what you think out there," my father said, and he spoke to Clyde, man to man, ignoring me. They were deeply serious all at once and absorbed into what I understood as the secret lives of men. It was important to watch them for clues.

My father acted as if he were just beginning to detail Clyde's real assignment. You might have thought we faced a mindless day spent riding that drag behind a farting old team. But no, it seemed Clyde's real mission involved a survey of conditions and experienced judgment.

"Them swales been coming to swamp grass," my father said. "We been drowning them out." He went on to talk about the low manure dams that spread irrigation water across the swales. Clyde would have the day to study those dams and figure out where they should be relocated.

Once we believed work done well would see us through. But it was not true. Once it seemed the rewards of labor would be naturally rationed out with at least a rough kind of justice, but we were unlettered and uninstructed in the true nature of our ultimate values. Our deep willingness to trust in our native goodness was not enough.

But we tried. This is a set of stories about that trying, called an apology because it is also a cautionary tale about learning to practice hardening of the heart. Even at the time I might have suspected my father wasn't much worried about swamp grass in the swales, and that Clyde Bolton knew he wasn't, and that it wasn't the point of their negotiations. My father was concerned about dignity, however fragile, as an ultimate value.

"Your father was the damndest son of a bitch," one of the ranch hands once told me. "He'd get you started on one thing, and make you think you were doing another thing that was more important, and then he would go off and you wouldn't see him for days, and pretty soon it was like you were working on your own place." It was not until I was a man in the job my father perfected that I learned the sandhill cranes were not endangered at all. It didn't matter. Those birds were exotic and lovely dancing their mating dances in our meadows as each circled the other with gawky tall-bird elegance, and balancing by their extended fluttering wings as they seized the impulse and looped across the meadows with their long necks extended to the sky and their beaks open to whatever ecstasy birds can know.

Sometimes I think my father made up the whole thing, and that he was simply trying to teach me and everyone else on the property that certain vulnerabilities should be cherished and protected at whatever inconvenience.

I have to wish there had been more such instructions, and that they had been closer to explicit. I wish he had passed along some detailed notion of how to be boss. It was a thing he seemed to do naturally. I wish he had made clear the dangers of posturing in front of people who are in some degree dependent on your whims, posturing until you are deep into the fraud of maintaining distance in place of authenticity. A man told me to smoke cigars. "They see you peel that cellophane," he said, "and they know you don't live like they do."

My father set up his Grain Camp on a sagebrush-hill slope beneath a natural spring on the west side of Warner Valley. And it was an encampment, short on every amenity except running water in the early days—a double row of one-room shacks, eight in all, trucked in from a nearby logging camp in the late 1930s. There were also two shacks tacked across each other in a T-shape to make a cookhouse: one for the cooking and another for the long table where everyone ate. The men lived two to a cabin in busy seasons, sweltering on that unshaded slope in the summers and waking in the night to the stink of drying work clothes as they fed split wood to their little stoves in the winter. They were a mix of transients and what we called homesteaders: men who stayed with us for more than an occasional season, often years in the same cabin that became known as theirs. Those men have my heart as I write this; they were my friends and my mentors; some of them died at the Grain Camp and have been inconspicuously dead for many years. Louie Hanson, Vance Beebe, Jake O'Rourke, Lee Mallard, so many others. I would like the saying of their names to be an act of pure celebration.

When I came home from the U.S. Air Force in the fall of 1957, I was twenty-five years old and back to beginnings after most of eight years away. I was a woeful figure from American business mythology, the boss's kid and heir to the property, soon to inherit, who didn't know anything. Then, in the spring of 1958, the myth came directly home to roost. I found myself boss at the Grain Camp, in my father's shoes.

There was no choice this side of disgrace but to plead justifiable ignorance and insinuate myself into the sympathies of the old hands. Ceremony demanded that I show up twice a day to sit at the head of the long table for meals, breakfast and noon, and in the course of those appearances legislate my way through the intricacies of managing 8,000 acres of irrigated land. For a long time I was bluffing, playing a hand I didn't understand, risking disgrace and reaping it plenty enough. The man who saved my bacon was an old alcoholic Swede in filthy coveralls named Louie Hanson, who sat at my right hand at the table.

About five-thirty or so on routine mornings, after a hot shower and instant coffee, I would drive the three or so miles to the Grain Camp. The best cabin, walls filled with sawdust for insulation, was where Louie lived. He had worked for my father since our beginnings in Warner. He hired out as a Cat skinner in 1937, to build dikes with a secondhand Caterpillar RD6, the first track-layer my father bought, and he made his way up to Cat mechanic, and into privileges, one of which was drinking.

Theoretically, we didn't allow any drinking at all. Period. Again, there were rules. You need to drink, go to town. Maybe your job will be waiting when you get back. Unless you were one of the old hands. Then your job was secure. But nobody was secure if they got to drinking on the job, or around camp.

Except for Louie. Every morning in winter he would go down to the Cat shop to build his fire before breakfast and dig a couple of beers from one of the bolt-rack cubbyholes, pop the tops, and set the bottles on the stove to heat. When they were steaming he would drink the beer in a few long draughts and be set to seize the day. So it would not be an entirely sober man I greeted when I came to breakfast and knocked on the door to his cabin. Resting on the greasy tarp that covered his bed, Louie would be squinting through the smoke from another Camel, sipping coffee from a filthy cup, and looking up to grin. "Hell, you own the place," he would say, "you're in."

Louie would blink his eyes. "Chee-rist. You got enough water in Dodson Lake?" He was talking about one of the grain fields we flooded every spring. And I wouldn't know. Did I have enough water in Dodson Lake? Louie would look at me directly. "Get a south wind and you are going to lose some dikes." I knew what that meant: eroded levee banks, washouts, catastrophe, 450 acres of flooded alfalfa.

Up at the breakfast table, while Louie reached for the pounded round steak, I would detail a couple of men to start drawing down the water in Dodson Lake—a process involving the opening of huge valves, pulling headgate boards, running the 18-inch pump. All of which would have been unnecessary if I had known what I was doing in the first place. Which everybody knew and nobody mentioned. All in all a cheap mistake, easily covered, wages and electricity to run the pump, wasted time, maybe a couple hundred bucks. Without Louie's intercession, maybe twenty thousand.

⌘

The deeply fearful are driven to righteousness, as we know, and they are the most fearsome fools we have. This is a story I have told as a tavern-table anecdote, in which I call our man The Murderer since I have no memory of his real name; it's a story called "The Day I Fired the Murderer." It's designed, as told in taverns, to make me appear ironic, liberated, and guilty no more, which implies there was guilt. And there was, in a double-bind sort of way that cornered me into thinking it was anger that drove me, and that my anger was justifiable.

I had been boss at the Grain Camp for four or five years, and I had come to understand myself as a young man doing good work, employing the otherwise unemployable (which was kind of true), and also as someone whose efforts were continually confounded by the incompetence of the men who worked for me. We were farming twenty-four hours a day through early May while the Canada honkers hatched their downy young and the tulips pushed up through the crusted flower beds and the Lombardy poplar broke their buds and the forsythia bloomed lurid yellow against the cookhouse wall. But I don't think of such glories when I remember those spring mornings. I remember the odor of dank peat turning up behind those disc Cats as we went on farming twenty-four hours a day, and how much I loved breaking ground.

Before sunrise on those mornings I would come awake and go piss, then stand in my undershorts on the screened-in veranda porch attached to the house where I lived with my wife and young children. I would shiver with chills and happiness as I smelled the world coming awake. Far out across our valley the lights on our D-7 disc Cats would flicker as lights do when seen through a screen, moving almost imperceptibly. I would take my binoculars and open the screen door and gaze out to those lights as if I might catch one of my night-shift Cat skinners at some dog-fuckery, but really all I wanted to see was the machinery moving. Those track-layers would clank along all through the hours of darkness at two or three miles an hour, turning a 36-foot swath, a 100 acres every night and another 100 acres on the day shift. The upturned soil would mellow in the air for a day, and then we would harrow and seal it with dust, and drill it to barley. In ten days or so the seedlings would break earth, and those orderly drill-rows undulating over the tilled ground toward the sundown light were softly yellow-green and something alive I had seen to completion.

It came to a couple hundred acres of barley every day for fifteen days, three thousand some odd acres in all. By the end of harvest in late September, at roughly a ton per acre, that came to 3,000 tons of barley at $50 a ton, or One Hundred and Fifty Thousand Dollars in the early 1960s, which was real money in our end of the world.

We drained the wetlands and thought that made them ours. We believed the world was made to be useful; we ditched and named the intersections of our ditches, Four Corners, the Big Pump, Center Bridge, and Beaty Bridge. We thought such naming made the valley ours. And we thought the people were ours.

The man I call The Murderer was one of those men who rode the disc Cats, circling toward the sunrise. My involvement with him started the previous fall when someone from the Oregon State Parole Board called and asked if we would participate in what they called their Custody Release Program. They would send us a parolee if we would guarantee a job; in return we got an employee who was forbidden to drink or quit, on penalty of being sent back to prison. If there was "anything," we could call and the state police would come take him away. It seemed like a correct idea; it had been twenty some years since The Murderer killed his wife in an act of drunken bewilderment he couldn't recall.

Frail and dark-eyed in a stiff new evergreen-colored work shirt with the sleeves rolled to expose thin white arms, pensive and bruised and looking incapable of much beyond remorse, The Murderer spent the winter feeding bales to the drag at our feed mill—a cold filthy job, and as monotonous an enterprise as it is possible to imagine this side of automation. So when it came time to go farming in the spring, I sat him up at the controls of a D-7, taught him to pull frictions and grease the rollers and called him a Cat skinner, which is to say, I gave him some power. The Murderer responded by starting to talk. His misinformed brightness chattered at the breakfast table.

All I remember is annoyance. Then it rained, and we couldn't work. My crew went off to town for a couple of days with my blessing. The Murderer went with them. That was against our rules, his and mine. He came back drunk, and I fired him on the spot. He was still drunk when he came up to breakfast; he was terribly frightened and unable to be sober, lowering himself into my mercies, which did not exist.

Only in the imagination can we share another person's specific experiences. I was the ice queen, which means no stories, please; there is no forgiveness for you and never will be, just roll your goddamned bed and be gone. If I fired him, he would go back to prison. I knew that. I am sure I imagined some version of his future—isolation again in his wrecked recognition that in this life he was not to be forgiven.

Stories bind us by reminding us that our lives all participate in the same fragilities, and thus demand we stay humane. But I didn't want to be humane; I wanted to be correct. If I had not ignored his devastation, as I no doubt saw or imagined it, I might have found a way to honor common sense and take him riding around with me that day as he sobered up, listening to his inane chatter. But I sent him down the road and thought I was doing the right thing. There were rules. As I tell the story I mean to say, See, I am not like that anymore. See. But we know that is only another strategy.

I fired a lot of men, and Louie Hanson more than once, after on-the-job binges. But Louie wouldn't go away; he saw the true nature of our contract. I needed his assurances exactly as he needed his life at the Grain Camp. After a few days Louie would sober up, and one morning he would be at the breakfast table as if nothing had happened. In fact he was fired the day he died.

He was too drunk to make sense by three in the afternoon and was feeding shots of whiskey to the chore man, which meant I had to take action. I told him to clear out. What he did was go off to visit a woman he had known in a small town just down into California.

"A fancy woman," Louie said after drawing himself up to fine old-man lewdness. "Screw you, I am going to see a woman I should have been seeing." He was seventy-seven years old and impossible to kill, so far as I knew, when he drove away in his old Plymouth, squinting through his cracked eyeglasses.

A stranger in a pickup truck hauled him home late in the night. Louie, who had wrecked the Plymouth, was ruined. He had a cut over one eye and was hallucinating as he lay curled into himself like an old knot, reeking with vomit, sick on the floor, unwilling to even open his eyes, and complaining that his eyeglasses were lost. This descent into nowhere had happened before. Let him lie. And he did, facing the wall for three days.

By then it was clear something terrible was afoot. Louie refused to hear of the hospital in Lakeview. They'll kill you, he said. Around the time of World War I, in the Imperial Valley of California near Calexico, his back had been broken when a bridge caved in under the weight of a steel-wheeled steam tractor. The doctors got him on morphine for the pain, and then fed him alcohol to get him off morphine, and that was it for the rest of his life, he said. Booze.

"They just left me there," he would say, half drunk and grinning as if it were a fine joke, "on the booze." He felt the doctors had already killed him. I called his son in Napa, California, who came overnight in an old car and talked Louie onto his feet, as I should have done, and into a trip over the Warner Mountains to the hospital.

All that should have been my responsibility. Days before, I should have ignored his wounded objections. The doctors wouldn't kill him, I knew it. He would have lived some more, not for long maybe, but some more. But such obligations were beyond my job description, and I fell back on excuses.

Louie Hanson died in the automobile, slumped sideways against his son. He died of a broken rib through one lung, which would have been fixable a day or so earlier. I went to the funeral, but wouldn't look in the coffin. There was nothing I wanted to know about the look of things in coffins. The year before, there had been an afternoon when I stood on a ditch bank with a dented bucket of softly orange carrot slices marinated in strychnine, poisoning badgers, dreading every moment I could foresee, all things equally unreal: my hand in the rubber glove holding the slice of carrot that was almost luminous, clouds over Bidwell Mountain, the sound of my breathing. I would have to move if I was ever going to get home. I was numb with dread and sorrowed for myself because I felt nothing but terror, and I had to know this was craziness. There is no metaphor for that condition; it is precisely like nothing.

By craziness I mean nearly catatonic fearfulness generated by the conviction that nothing you do connects to any other particular thing inside your life. Mine was not real craziness, although some fracturing of ice seemed to lie just around the corner of each moment. It was easy to imagine vanishing into complete disorientation. My trouble could be called "paralyzed before existential realities," a condition I could name, having read Camus like any boy of my time. But such insight was useless. Not one thing was valuable unless it helped toward keeping the lid on my own dis-ease.

Fee Point reaches into the old tule beds on the east side of Warner. A homesteader shack out there was my father's first Grain Camp cookhouse, in 1938. I see my young mother at that encampment in a soft summery wind, wearing a yellow cotton dress and gazing out to plow-ground fields being cut from the swamps. Close to thirty years later my Cat skinners crushed that shack into a pile of weathered junk lumber, dumped on diesel, and burned it. It was January, and we warmed our hands on the flames, then turned away to a salamander stove and drank steaming coffee and ate cold roast-beef sandwiches sent out from another cookhouse.

In Latin *familia* means residence and family, which I take to mean community, an interconnection of stories. As I lie down to sleep I can stand at the Fee Place and see my mother and—many years later—those Cat skinners and that homestead house burning. It's an example of the ways we are inhabited by stories, and the ways they connect.

Waterbirds were a metaphor for abundance beyond measure in my childhood. A story about waterbirds: on a dour November afternoon, my father sat on a wooden case of shotgun shells in the deep tules by Pelican Lake like a crown prince of shotgunning, and dropped 123 ducks for an Elks Club feed. The birds were coming north to water from the grain fields and fighting a stiff headwind. The birds flared and started to settle, just over him, and they would not stop coming into the long red flame from his shotgun as darkness came from the east. Dead birds fell, collapsed to the water, and washed to shore in the wind. Eventually it was too dark to shoot, and the dead birds were heaped in the back of his pickup, and he hauled them to town. Having discharged a civic duty, he dumped them off with the woman he had hired to do the picking and went on to a good clear-hearted night at the poker table.

When someone had killed too many birds, their necks were strung together with baler twine, and they were hung from spikes in a crab-apple tree back of our house. There, they froze, and were given away to anyone who might come visiting. When the time came for you to leave, we would throw in three or four Canada honkers as a leave-taking gift, stiff as cordwood, and give you the name of the lady in town who did the picking. What is the crime here?

It is not my father's. In later years men came to me and told me he was the finest man they ever worked for, and I envy that fineness, by which, I think they meant fair and convivial—and just, in terms of an implied contract. From an old hand who had worked for room and board and no wages through the Great Depression that was a kind of ultimate praise. They knew he hadn't broken any promises, and he had sense enough to know that finally you can't really help anybody die, no matter how much you owe them. But there was an obvious string of crimes. Maybe we should have known the world wasn't made for our purposes, to be remodeled into our idea of an agricultural paradise, and that Warner Valley wasn't there to have us come along to drain the swamps, and level the peat ground into alfalfa land. No doubt we should have known the waterbirds would quit coming. But we had been given to understand that the places we owned were to be used as we saw fit. The birds were part of all that.

What went wrong? Rules of commerce, or cowardice, or what? Bad thinking? Failure to identify what was sacred? All of the above? Did such failures lead me to treat men as if they were tools, to be used? Probably. But that is no excuse for participating in the kind of coldheartedness we see everywhere, the crime we commit while we all claim innocence.

One night in Lakeview I was dancing with a woman we knew as the Crop-Duster's Wife. She came to the taverns every night, and she was beautiful in an overbruised sort of way, but she wouldn't go find a bed with any of us. She was, she claimed, married forever to a man who was off in Arkansas dusting cotton from an old Steerman bi-wing. She said she just hoped he didn't wreck that Steerman into some Arkansas church. We sat at the bar. I was drunk and told her about Louie Hanson and how he died, eager to confess my craziness. Maybe I thought a woman who waited for a man who flew crop-dusting aircraft would understand. Maybe I thought she would fall for a crazy man.

"There is nothing to dislike but the meanness," she said, picking at her words. "You ought to be glad you ever knew those old farts." Failures of sympathy, she was saying, originate in failures of imagination, which is a betrayal of self. Like many young men, I could only see myself in the mirror of a woman. Offering the utility of that reflection, and a degree of solace, was understood to be the work of women; their old job was to inhabit the house and forgive, at least until they got tired of it. In those days a woman who wanted to be done with such duties might buy herself a wedding ring and make up a story about a man who flew his Steerman every morning to support her. That woman might say people like me were no cure for loneliness. Then she might excuse my self-centered sorrowing, and say we don't have any choice, it's the creatures we are. She might tell me to wise up and understand that sympathy is useful only when it moves us to give up on the distances we maintain, our barricades, and the coldness of our hearts. It's possible to imagine a story in which The Murderer doesn't return to the Oregon State Prison, but lives at the Grain Camp until he has forgiven himself and healed—a humorous old man you could turn to for sensible advice. In the end we would all be forgiven. We would have learned to let the birds fly away because it is not necessarily meat we are hunting.

Leaving the Ranch

DURING THE 1960s I became someone else, a man moving toward a new and different life. There were defeats and evasions and happenstance insights, one and another until I was the next person.

In late February, spring runoff from the Warner Mountains would begin. Deep Creek and Twenty Mile would come muddy on the dark cold mornings—spitting rain—and there were miles of muddy levee banks to patrol before breakfast. I had pumps and headgates to check. Rotten conditions, more so if you fooled around and got stuck before daybreak and had to walk out for help. But I never used up my patience with getting the work done. Some rewards of farming I loved until the day I left. On late May evenings, after supper, the dishes stacked in the sink, my wife and daughter and son and I would load into my blue 1961 Ford pickup and drive ranch roads through the wild meadows and willows along sloughs where the redwing blackbirds flocked with occasional teals and mallards with their young in the mossy water. We were off to see the crops. The sun would be down near the rim, which turned black in shadow. Faraway lights shone from our kitchen and from the homes of people we had neighbored with most of our adult lives. We sighted down the drill-rows of barley seedlings, backlit and luminous against dark peat soils. It seemed this ought to be enough to sustain us, always.

⁓

But my pilgrimage toward leaving had long since begun. It started with my mother. The daughter of a power-company blacksmith in Klamath Falls, like many small-town women, she took piano and voice lessons. She was quick and pretty and good at her music and yearned not so much to escape as to live a life of consequence. I bless her. She helped me to the notion that there were valuable lives to be lived outside ranching (not an altogether common admission in our neck of the woods).

My father, I think, never voluntarily read a novel or saw a movie in his entire life. But he loved the idea of Lewis and Clark. He regretted missing out on the days when the West was, as he thought of it, stone fresh and new. My mother aspired to sing opera, and learned to interest herself in cultural matters, which is likely the reason she belonged to the Book-of-the-Month Club and accounts for the copy of *The Big Sky* at our house in Warner Valley. Maybe she ordered it with the hope that my father would spend some nights reading, meditating on the mountain-man glories he had missed. But he was a man in the power of his life and more inclined to spend winter nights testing his genius at the poker table.

Then, the summer of 1948, when I was sixteen, bored in a schoolboy way, prime for enlightenment or love, I found the book and fell into it. In the hayfield I would sing pop ballads at top volume and daydream about the Rockies Front. After work, I would shower, eat, and sit under a light on the screened veranda, eager to fall again in with those doomed romantic wayfarers, Boone and Teal Eye and Dick Summers. I envied the man who wrote the book and wondered what it would be like to know so much, in complex detail, about the plants and animals and rivers and mountains that inhabited the place where you lived (each "thing" interwoven with all else), and how people could emerge from words. I'm not sure I learned any politics after that summer.

The Big Sky was an important discovery for an isolated ill-educated boy. Through it I began to intuit that our lives, so far in the outback of the American West, were connected to the rest of America and history. Stories, I began to understand, help you understand your place in the world and even help you come to believe in the importance of your own life.

A doorway into serious reading had been opened through the efforts of a teacher my junior year in Klamath Union High School. That sainted man drove a crowd of semi-jocks to memorize some James Whitcomb Riley and Emerson and Whitman; he tricked us; and he got me to enjoy it, to come away thinking poetry was a thing I liked. So I was happy, the beginning of my freshman year at Oregon State, when I'd signed up for a class in Introduction to Literature. The first thing we read was Eudora Welty's "The Death of a Traveling Salesman." Grown-up reading turned out to be incomprehensible, another defeat.

It's hard to understand why I was so baffled by a story that seems quite direct. "Bowman could not speak. He was shocked with knowing what was really in this house. A marriage, a fruitful marriage. That simple thing. Anyone could have had that." Given my family, it's possible, in my seventeen-year-old beginnings, that I simply did not understand much about the idea of a fruitful marriage.

Then, and they seem connected, another breakaway, my own early marriage. What we thought we were going to do, my wife and I, in our beginning, was get each and every one thing right, never make any mistakes, so long as we lived. But we found reasons to ignore the chances of giving ourselves away to each other. I wish I could say it was because we didn't try. But it wasn't anything so simple. We worked hard at being generous and good and thought that meant we were being good to the world. It seemed to work for a long time. We thought ours was the special case. Our connection would never fail. But we've been divorced for many years. What did we ask of each other that was too much? In what ways did our inabilities manifest themselves? Maybe we were too careful and tried to be too good.

In December of 1951, when we were nineteen, we were quite formally married, after religious instruction. She wore a long white dress, and I, a white college-boy dinner jacket. The ceremony took place in a fine hardwood Presbyterian church. We spent our first night in the Eugene Hotel. The next day we visited the Sea Lion Caves. We were children, strangers, but we were decent children, and we tried to accommodate each other.

Here it began. She worked Christmas vacation checking groceries for Safeway. I rested on the couch in our student apartment and read Henry Steele Commager's two-volume *History of the United States* cover to cover. This was strange ground: I was a married man; I was supposed to be looking for work, but I had never read a book like that, never before—a book with so many pages and so serious and filled with things I didn't know. I started making lists of Civil War battles; I couldn't stop. That was a first experience with my own ignorance, my recognition that my education had been appalling. I knew nothing of the "great world," not much about ranching, nothing much about the farming in which my father had made his reputation. At Oregon State there were professors of agriculture who would lecture the class about my father's avant-garde irrigation practices and turn to me for answers to their questions. I didn't know what they were talking about. Now I could not stop reading. I was married and should have been working. I felt guilt, but I went on reading and began one of the retreats of my life, which I have to respect, I think, as a move, however neurotic, toward salvation.

As illiterate boys will, I came to books, and learned to value ideas beyond anything actual that might be happening right at the time. I reread *Moby-Dick* and *Walden* and the Cornford translation of *The Republic* three times in my senior year at Oregon State, as if I thought they needed to be memorized. But the story that moved me most fiercely was the *Iliad.* French critic Simone Weil has written, "The true hero, the true subject, the center of the *Iliad* is force. [For those] who perceive force, today as yesterday, at the very center of human history, the *Iliad* is the purest and the loveliest of mirrors." Weil might have been writing about me. "Thus they celebrated the funeral games of Hector, Breaker of Horses." That was the final line, in my prose translation of the *Iliad.* Following combat, and the death of a great hero, those ancient people ultimately celebrated the fact that he had been a breaker of horses. The people in the *Iliad* and the people I had grown up around in Warner Valley were alike in their regard for horsemen.

Books piled up like barricades as I turned from my friends and their athletics and became the worst sort of school-boy pedant. Those years were time out from life. My wife checked groceries while I took money from my father and worked at small jobs for the research agencies connected to Oregon State. I hoed beets in long rows, things like that, while the books were my obsession and my sickness, a king-dom where nobody lived but me, a place made of ideas. It's a place where I still do my living much of the time. While it's not a real place, for a long while it was my main place to go, a hideout. The best trick of my life was turning what I did there into work and a justifiable profession.

The idea of writing came to me at that time. Maybe it started with my incapacities and failures at what were thought of as mannish things in my part of creation. Maybe I wanted a world in which I was the one who made it up. Maybe it was power I was after.

The man who got me back to books in college was Herbert Childs, an English professor. I respected his intelligence in the same way I allowed my father his authority. Childs nearly wept in our class when Adlai Stevenson was defeated by Eisenhower: "The last good man who will ever run for president," he said. Maybe he was right. His performance seemed overcooked to a boy from eastern Oregon, unmanly. I looked away. But in my heart I agreed. I was prime in my readiness to abandon the politics of my family.

My wife's father pressed me to read Hemingway. I loved poor sad Hemingway, which makes my conjectures about masculine failure and a yearning for power seem accurate. I thought I'd found a writer who spoke of what I understood to be actualities and urgencies, like the possibility of a boy like me dying in Korea. Hemingway touched a run of desire to say things that were never to be horseshit. If you followed that lead you might not have to think you'd wasted your life as you died. So I thought. (It made reports of his death by shotgun hard to accept.) The hard part was figuring out which things to say. I tried writing stories. All the people in them were doomed. I took a class from Bernard Malamud, and there I found that intellectuals were a breed I hadn't imagined. Malamud met with us in a Quonset hut, and he was happy, I think. He'd just published *The Natural.* After teaching Freshman Comp for years, five classes, he'd been rewarded with four classes of Comp, plus Creative Writing. Right off he encouraged us to write something reeking slightly of the actual world. I wrote up rancher anecdotes I thought of as indeed just like life. He told us about recognitions and the fact that narratives wouldn't become stories until something changes, until the consequences of some stance had played out. He said there had to be recognitions, times of seeing the world in fresh ways. That's how stories worked, he said, what they were about, coming to see freshly. But I already knew true things about the world and had no need of recognitions. So I thought in my boyish arrogance. One true thing I thought I saw was that Malamud, in an outlander way, was attempting to subvert my Warner Valley understandings. I wanted none of his nonsense and wrote long drifty anecdotes. Malamud gave me a series of flunks, big red F after red F, until, with contempt for both of us, I wrote a story with rising action and a recognition—a college love story. Malamud gave me a big red A. What a pain in the ass I must have been. How that poor man must have shook his head over my ignorance. But they hooked me, Bernard and Hemingway. What a combo. I was set to be a writer; that was it for me.

And then, at the age of twenty-one, in January of 1954, I graduated from Oregon State in General Agriculture. It's hard to imagine a more useless degree unless you have it in mind to spend a life as a county agent deep in the Willamette Valley. Soldiers were dying in Korea, and my wife had got herself pregnant (however childlike it seems, that was how I thought of pregnancy, as a thing women did for mysterious reasons). So, feeling I had no choice, I enlisted in the Air Force where I was unlikely ever to see combat in what I understood to be utterly pointless warfare. We had to put off our lives for another four years, that was the thinking.

Our daughter, Karen, was born while I was in basic training in Texas. I brought my wife to join me in Denver, where I was in Photo Intelligence School. We moved on to Travis AFB in California, where our son Bradley was born, and I worked for the Strategic Air Command. Then we went to Guam. Eventually my time in the military was over. What now?

Back to the ranch. A clear mistake, yet it was all I could imagine. By late 1961 I'd gotten lost in a double-bind collapse. It felt like simple, terrifying all-day-long craziness. I wasn't trying to write, although, attempting to save myself, I was always intending to be a writer: I was trying to be someone else. Off on running drunks, incapacitated by the ongoing hangover, I was trying to read philosophy I couldn't make sense of—Kant and Alfred North Whitehead—while really understanding the world in terms of Hank Williams, "Why don't you love me like you used to do?"

Nodding my head in dimwitted agreement with Camus, I was terrified by *The Magic Mountain*, subscribed to the the *New York Times Book Review*, the *Kenyon Review*, the *Sewanee Review*, the *Hudson* and *Virginia Quarterly* reviews; I ordered eight or ten deeply serious books a month from San Francisco (we lived far away from bookstores). Hungering over the meager collections shelved in stationery stores when I got to town, I was a man with a family, but close to paralyzed by the fact that I no longer wanted any life that I could imagine as possibly mine. Why couldn't family and work and property be enough?

Those last years on the ranch, driving the 17-mile levee bank around the east side of the valley in midsummer, I began to recognize the malaise that drove me to leave. Left of the narrow roadway, barley in the expanse of Huston Swamp was ripening toward harvest, green fading to yellow. On the other side, the "outside" we called it, lay an alkaline flat where floodwaters, backed up from the levee, had drowned sage and greasewood and reached maybe a half-mile toward a rise of scab rock and the eventual deserts of Nevada. The ripeness of that field and that expanse of alkali shimmering in the heat, they were otherwise motionless—a condition I saw as empty.

Leaning on the tailgate of my Ford pickup, I became aware that this valley, where I had always thought of myself as living, had gone silent in some terrible way. I was frightened even though I'd read *Silent Spring* and knew what had happened. We'd mechanized the ancient, seven- or eight-thousand-year-old animal-centered labor of farming into agribusiness, and through "unintended consequences" had deadened the life of the valley. In this memory there are no birds calling, not even the sounds of insects. Miles away, dust rose in twisting strings behind our three-wire New Holland balers. Like so many young people who grow up isolated from what their culture defines as significant, I felt cut off from the Great World in irrevocable ways and driven to the idea that whatever I did know was of little interest to much of anyone out there.

But those days weren't altogether doomed. Twilight would go luminous. Our children, on a concrete irrigation dam, were silhouetted against that light. The water between us curled with places where fish might live. Those children waited on the irrigation dam as I continued fishing, while darkness came down. I didn't know how much it mattered—that moment in which fishing was all I was doing. They were waiting for me to get done with it and go home and sit at our table and look across to my wife and have a drink of whiskey. How much from that moment, that instant, our children, me with their mother, do I remember? How long would it take to name the little I do know about what was going on, since this was from a time when I thought I was crazy and unable to know anything?

Why wasn't I paying attention? Who were we? It isn't

my business to guess what my wife thought. We argued in the traditional ways. She was angry, and betrayed, and stayed humane. She tried to help, but I wouldn't let her. It was beyond me to admit that I needed help.

The cure took a long while. An accumulating intention began to become resolve, and on the day after Thanksgiving, 1965, when I was thirty-three years old, I started trying to write. Determined that I'd work at it every day, give it a life-time effort whether it worked or not because success wasn't the point, I would get out of bed before sunup, type an hour or so, and then go off to work. I didn't know what I was at-tempting. I thought it was about sentences and paragraphs, fashioning elegances out of what you already knew. I didn't yet see that writing like any art is chancing to know freshly. As such it's always worth doing; it's worth finding gestures that suggest understandings.

☙

But my arty inclinations might never have been strong enough to get me off the ranch. They needed to be pushed by economics. It began when, in solemn conclave, in the mid-1960s, my family voted to sell the MC. Ours was a shirtsleeves-to-shirtsleeves-in-three-generations family. My grandfather, it was said, "finally got his name on that prop-erty and them grandkids will piss it away. Count on it."

The folk-talk was accurate, not that it took a genius to foresee that future. Most of us wanted out, for simple reasons having to do with money and freedom. What we owned was not land but shares in what was called "The Warner Valley Livestock Company." The story might have come out differently if each of us had owned some land—individually—acres we could walk around on and dig in. We might have felt ourselves connected to living items like nesting ring-necked Manchurian pheasants. We might have talked about how we might live on our place, since talk is an aphrodisiac and way of holding people to the soil. But most of us didn't own land, and our shares did not, as a matter of policy, pay any dividends. Profits went back into the property, a fine deal if you were a majority stockholder with tax problems, but not so hot for minority stockholders who might want to control their money or maybe piss it away on racehorses or trips to Tibet.

As a rule, even to family members, the Warner Valley Livestock Company paid salaries. If you worked for the company, you got a salary. If not, you didn't get, as is said, shit. So it came to be that various relatives, who were unlikely to ever be employed in the ranch business, thought they'd rather have their money invested in a shoe store or in Dairy Queens, or blow it on frivolity if they damned well pleased. At family gatherings such desires were labeled cheap and common and foolish. Since I was one of those getting a salary, it took me awhile to realize I was also a heretic; I wanted out. People ask me if I don't wish I were back on the ranch. Yeah, I say, I have a deep yearning to trail after cows and pitch hay and live hundreds of miles from a good bookstore. The answer is always no.

I have a life that is mine. I, to some degree, made it up. That other life, in serious ways, belonged to somebody's grandson. I was lucky to get out.

By 1967 it became obvious that we were at last going to sell the property in Warner. Another chance at a new life loomed. So what would it be this time? Chaos, it seemed. My wife and children left for California. There was not a thing to do but carry on. I had made this mess, so I had to see it through. Nothing remained in the house but my books and some ashtrays. The spaces echoed. A friend came to help me box the books. "Jesus Christ," he said. "You'd be a smart son of a bitch if you read all these." What did he think I was doing with them? Who, through my conceal-ments, had I led him to believe that I was? Even my friends didn't know me. I wasn't surprised as I drove off alone to work on properties we owned a hundred miles away, on the Klamath Marsh.

My brother and I, that fall, would take an old World War II jeep and patch fences. Enormous yellow pine stank of sweet pitch while we leaned against them and ate our lunch and listened to the World Series on a portable radio. We hammered staples as contrails crossed in the skies. The highway was thirty miles to the west. As winter came I tried to relearn the arts of horseback. I rode frozen swamplands for cattle.

In December the snow was two feet deep. I was holed up in a ranch-hand house on a bank overlooking the iced-up Williamson River. Ponderosa pine sighed in the winds. I listened to country music on my radio, trying to cherish a future in which this would all be grist for the mill, when one morning my father drove in sort of grandly for that neck of the deep woods in a new yellow Mercedes, accompanied by the good woman who was his second wife. He parked with the motor running, fog lifting from the tailpipe into the bright ten-below-zero sunlight, and came to the house alone, and asked me if I had anything to drink, by which he meant whiskey. What I had was Jack Daniel's. I poured him a glass, and he asked what I was going to do with myself. I told him that I'd be leaving after the first of the year, off to college, to studies in creative writing, which was not a dis-cipline anybody ever heard of in our part of the world. He looked at me as if I were crazy and sipped at his tumbler of whiskey. "I spent a lot of my life at things I hated," he said. "I sure as hell wouldn't recommend that." Then he changed the subject. We talked about shipping cattle off the frozen meadows.

What I think he was saying had to do with the fact that he had once wanted to be a lawyer and had been talked out of that ambition by his father. I think he was reminding me that his life of working with his father had been a failure. My father was sixty-eight. He had undergone a divorce, five heart attacks, and a stroke. He was married again, and he was telling me to get on with my own opportunities. That thought has heartened me through the years from then to now.

Reimagining Warner

A SCAB-HANDED WANDERING CHILD who rode off on old horses named Snip and Moon, I grew up with the thronging presence of animals. Sundays in the summer my family would spread their blankets by Twenty Mile Creek and let us kids catch as many rainbow trout as we could stand. Sandhill cranes danced their courtship dances in our meadows. Feral hogs inhabited the swampland tule beds and would eat the downy young of Canada geese if they could, but never caught them so far as I knew. The haying and feeding and cow herding couldn't have been done without horses. We only lived the life we had with the help of horses.

Warner Valley, tucked against an enormous reach of Great Basin sagebrush and lava desert in southeastern Oregon and northern Nevada, was a hidden world. Land-locked waters flow down from the mountains to the west, but don't find a way out to the sea. They accumulate and evaporate in shallow lakes named Pelican, Crump, Hart, Stone Corral, and Bluejoint.

The late 1930s, when I was a child in that valley, were like the last years of the nineteenth century. What I want to get at is isolation. We were thirty-six gravel-road miles over the Warner Mountains from the lumbering and rancher town of Lakeview (maybe 2,500 souls). Warner Valley was not on the route to anywhere. The way in was the way out. The deserts to the east were traced with wagon-track roads over the salt-grass playas and around rim rocks from spring to spring, waterhole to waterhole, but nobody ever headed in that direction with the idea of going toward the future. To the east lay deserts and more deserts. From a ridge above our buckaroo camp beside the desert spring at South Corral, we could see the long notched snowy ridge of Steens Mountain off in the eastern distances; this was the high country where the whores from Burns went in summer to camp with the sheepherders amid aspen trees at a place called Whorehouse Meadows. Nobody but wandering men ever went there; men who would never be around when you needed them. And beyond, toward Idaho, more desert.

We had control of a huge acreage in Warner. My father was making serious progress at draining the swamplands. The spring of 1946 my grandfather traded off close to two hundred work teams for chicken feed. He replaced those horses with a fleet of John Deere tractors. Harnesses rotted in the barns until the barns were torn down. I wonder if my grandfather and father understood how irrevocably they were giving up what they seemed to care about more than anything when they talked of happiness—their lives in conjunction to animals. I wonder why they acted as if they didn't care. Maybe they thought the animals were immortal. I recall those great teams of workhorses running the hayfields in summer before daybreak. Their hooves would echo on the sod as we herded them toward the willow corral at some hay camp through morning mists. The boy I was knew at least enough to know he loved them and how that love was reason to revere everything in sight for another morning. Those massive horses were like mirrors in which I could see my emotions reflected. If they loved the world, and they seemed to, on mornings when our breaths fogged before us, so did I.

After World War II, electricity from Bonneville Power came to Warner, and telephones that sort of functioned. The road over the mountains and down along Deep Creek was paved, and our work in the fields had in so many ways gone mechanical. Eventually we had television. Our isolation was dissolving.

About then I watched the first Beatles telecast, and in the early 1960s, chamber of commerce gentlemen from Winnemucca got together with like-minded gents from Lakeview. They decided it made economic sense to punch a highway across the deserts between those two cities. Think of the tourists. The two-lane asphalt ran north from Winnemucca to Denio, then turned west to cross the million or so acres of rangeland we leased from the Bureau of Land Management (we saw those acreages as ours, as if we owned them: in those days we virtually did), over an escarpment called the Dougherty Slide, across Guano Valley and down Greaser Canyon, and directly through our meadowlands in Warner Valley.

I recall going out to watch the highway-building as it proceeded, the self-important recklessness of those men at their work, the roaring of the D-7 Caterpillars and the clouds of dust rising behind the huge careening of the self-propelled scrapers; and I remember being excited, full up with pride because the great world was at last coming to us in Warner Valley. Not that it did. Traffic flow never amounted to much. Maybe it will, one of these days.

Enormous changes were sweeping our world. We didn't want to encounter hippies or revolutionaries on the streets in Lakeview. Or so we said. But like anybody, we yearned to be in on the action.

We were delighted, one 4th of July, to hear that the Hells Angels motorcycle gang from Oakland had headed across the deserts north to Winnemucca on their way to a weekend of kicking ass in Lakeview, and that they had been turned back by a single deputy sheriff. The long string of lowriders were coming on the two-lane blacktop across the one of the desert swales, and the deputy, all by himself, stood there by his Chevrolet. A slight, balding man, he had flagged down the leaders, and they'd had a talk. "Nothing I can do about it," the deputy said, "but they're sighting in their deer rifles. These boys, they mean to sit back there three hundred yards and shoot you off them motorcycles. They won't apologize or anything. You fellows are too far out in the country."

According to legend, the leaders of the Hells Angels decided the deputy was right: they knew they were way out in the country, and they turned back. I've never talked to anybody who knew if that story were true, but we loved it. It was a story that told us we were capable of defending ourselves and not altogether powerless in a nation we understood to be going on without us. We never doubted some of our southeastern Oregon boys would have shot those Hells Angels off their bikes. Some places were still big and open enough to be safe from outsiders.

During the great flood in December of 1964, when the Winnemucca-to-the-Sea Highway acted like a dam across the valley by backing up water over four or five thousand acres, my brother Pat walked a D-7 Caterpillar out along the asphalt and cut the highway three or four times, deep cuts so the floodwaters could pour through and drain away north. What he liked best, Pat said, was socking that bulldozer blade down and ripping up that asphalt with the yellow lines painted on it. We were still our own people.

Huge and open to anything as southeastern Oregon may have seemed in those old days, it was also inhabited by spooks. In autumn of the same year the Winnemucca-to-the-Sea Highway came across our meadowlands, I had our heavy equipment, our Carry-All scrapers and D-7 bull-dozers, at work on a diversion canal we were cutting through three hundred yards of sage-covered sandhills at the south end of Warner, rerouting Twenty Mile Creek. Soon they were turning up bones—human bones, lots of them. I recall a clear October afternoon and those white bones scattered in the gravel, and my Cat skinners standing there beside their idling machines, perplexed and unwilling to continue. "Ah, hell, never mind," I said. "Crank 'em up." There wasn't a thing to do but keep rolling. Bones from an ancient Indian burial ground were sacred, but so was our work, more so as I saw it. My Cat skinners threatened to quit. I told them I'd give them a ride to town, where I'd find plenty of men who would welcome the work. They didn't quit. I ducked my head so I couldn't see and drove away. If you're baking a cake, you have to break some eggs. That was a theory we knew about. We thought we were doing God's work. We were cultivating, creating order, and what we liked to think of as a version of Paradise. That work was like art, always there, always in need of improving, doing, and a pleasure. It's reassuring, so long as the work is not boring, to wake up and find your task is still there, your tools still in the tunnel. You can lose a life in the work. People do.

⚬

But we left, we quit, in a run of family trouble. People ask if I don't feel a great sense of loss, cut off from the valley and methods of my childhood. The answer is no. Nothing much has changed when I go back. The rim above the valley lies black against the sunset light as it did when I was a child. The topography of my dreams, I like to think, is still in-tact. But that's nonsense. We did great damage to the valley as we pursued our sweet impulse to create an agribusiness paradise. The rich peat ground began to go saline, the top layer blew away. We drilled in chemical fertilizers along with our barley seed and sprayed with 2-4-D Ethyl and Parathion (which killed even the songbirds). But birds can be thought of as *charismatic megafauna.* We all worry about birds. Forms of life we didn't even know about were equally threatened. *Catostomus warnerensis,* the Warner sucker, was endangered. So were eight other fish species, seven plant species, and seven plant communities such as *Poptri/corstosalix,* a riparian plant community centered on black cottonwood, red osier dogwood, and willow.

As a child I loved to wander animal trails through dense brush by the creeks, where the ring-necked Manchurian pheasants and egg-eating racoons and stalking lynx cats traveled. I wonder about colonies of red osier dogwood and black cottonwood. I was often among them, at times curled up and asleep in the dry grass as I shared in their defenselessness and didn't know it. The way my family and I built canals in order to contain the wildness of the valley and regulate the ways of water to our own uses must have been absolutely destructive to the Warner sucker, a creature we would not have valued at all—tiny, slippery, and useless, thus valueless. I sent my gang of Caterpillar bulldozers to clean out brush along stretches of creek side thick with red osier dogwood and black cottonwood. Let in light, let the grass grow, feed for the livestock— that was the theory. Maybe we didn't really abandon those creatures in that valley; perhaps we mostly destroyed them before we left. We did enormous damage in the thirty some years that we were there. Countrysides like the Dordogne and Umbria and Tuscany, which have been farmed thousands of years, look to be less damaged. But maybe that's because the serious kill-off took place so long ago.

I love Warner as a child loves its homeland, and some sense of responsibility for what's there stays with me. Or maybe I'm trying to feel good about myself.

But that's what we all want to do, isn't it? It's my theory that everyone yearns, as we did in Warner by plowing those swamps, with all that bulldozing, to make a positive effect in the world. But how to keep from doing harm? Sometimes that seems to be the only question. We have to act. To do so responsibly we ought to examine our desires. What do we really want?

I went to Warner with a couple of filmmakers from NBC. Some footage ran on the *Today Show*. Sitting in a GMC pickup truck alongside a bulldozed reef of chemically contaminated cow shit outside feedlot pens where fat cattle existed like creatures in a machine, I found it in myself to say the valley should be given back to the birds and turned into a wildlife refuge.

It was a way of saying good-bye, saying the biological health of the valley was more important than the well-being of the community of ranchers who lived there. I had gone to grade school with some of them. It was an act people living in Warner mostly understood as betrayal.

Some eggs were indeed broken, but I had at last gotten myself to say what I believed. Around 1990, when I heard that our ranch in Warner along with two others out in the deserts to the east were for sale, and that the Nature Conservancy was interested, I was surprised by the degree to which I was moved and excited. Maybe, I thought, this would be a second chance at paradise in my heartland, an actual shot at reimagining desire. What did I really want? A process, everybody involved—ranchers and people from the towns, conservationists—all taking part in that reimagining. I wanted them to each try defining the so-called land of their heart's desiring, the way they would if they were running the world. I wanted them to compare their versions of paradise and notice again the ways we all want so many of the same things—like companionship in a community of people we respect and meaningful work. I hoped they might get started on the painstaking work of a practical plan for making their visions of the right life come actual, a plan for using, restoring, and preserving the world I grew up in. I liked to imagine pumps and dikes and headgates would be torn out in Warner, and that swamps might go back to tules. That's my idea of progress—re-create habitat for the waterbirds and the tiny, less charismatic creatures. But nothing like that has happened. The Nature Conservancy did not buy the land. The MC Ranch, our once-upon-a-time property in Warner, was stripped of livestock and machinery and sold to what I understand as a consortium of ranchers. I have no idea of their plans—they don't confide in me, the turncoat.

But the world is inevitably coming to Warner Valley and the surrounding deserts. The BLM purchased thousands of acres of prime hay land in north Warner and included it in a management unit in which no grazing is allowed. The idea of the federal government buying land and taking it out of production (out of the tax base) was unthinkable when I lived in Warner. The old drift fences on Hart Mountain were torn out. Again, no more grazing.

There's no use sighting in the scopes on deer rifles, not anymore. This invasion will not be frightened away. There's nothing for the people in my old homeland to do but work out an accommodation with the thronging, invading world.

So many of our people, in the old days of the American West, came seeking a fold in time, a hideaway where they and generations after them could be at home. Think of *familia*, hearth and home fire, the fishing creek where it falls out of the mountains into the valley, and the Lombardy poplar beside the white house, and the orchard where children run in sweet clover under blossoming apple trees. But that's my paradise, at least as I remember it, not yours. We have taken the West for about all it has to give. We have lived like children, taking and taking for generations, and now that childhood is over. It's time we gave something back to the natural systems of order that have supported us—some care and tenderness, which is the most operative notion I think—tenderness. Our isolations are gone, in the West and everywhere. We need to give time to the arts of cherishing the things we adore before they have simply vanished. Maybe it will be like learning a skill: how to live in paradise.

Redneck Secrets

Back in my more scattered days there was a time when I decided the solution to all life's miseries would begin with marrying a nurse. Cool hands and commiseration. She would be a second-generation Swedish girl who left the family farm in North Dakota to live a new life in Denver; her hair would be long and silvery blond; and she would smile every time she saw me and always be after me to get out of the house and go have a glass of beer with my buckaroo cronies.

Our faithfulness to each other would be legendary. We would live near Lolo, Montana, on the banks of the Bitterroot River where Lewis and Clark camped to rest on their way west. "Traveler's Rest" is land that floods a little in the spring of the year, a small price to pay for such connection with mythology. Our garden would be intricately perfect on the sunny uphill side of our sixteen acres, with little wooden flume boxes to turn the irrigation water down one ditch or another.

We would own three horses, one a blue roan Appaloosa, and haul them around in our trailer to jackpot roping events on summer weekends. I wouldn't be much good on horseback, never was, but nobody would care. The saddle shed would be tacked to the side of our double-wide expando New Moon mobile home, and there would be a neat little lawn with a white picket fence about as high as your knee, and a boxer dog called Aces and Eights, with a great studded collar. There would be a .357 magnum pistol in the drawer of the bedside table, and on Friday night we would dance to the music of old-time fiddlers at some country tavern and in the fall we would go into the mountains for firewood and kill two or three elk for the freezer. There would be wild asparagus along the irrigation ditches and morels down under the cottonwood by the river, and we would always be good.

And I would keep a journal, like Lewis and Clark, and spell bad because in my heart I would want to be a mountain man—"We luved aft the movee in the bak seet agin tonite."

∞

We must not gainsay such Western dreams. They are not automatically idiotic. There are, after all, good Rednecks and bad Rednecks. Those are categories.

So many people in the American West are hurt, and hurting. Bad Rednecks originate out of hurt and a sense of having been discarded and ignored by the Great World, which these days exists mostly on television, distant and most times dizzily out of focus out here in Redneck country.

Bad Rednecks lose faith and ride away into foolishness, striking back. The spastic utility of violence. The other night in a barroom, I saw one man turn to another who had been pestering him with drunken nonsense. "Son," he said, "you better calm yourself, because if you don't, things are going to get real Western here for a minute."

∞

Real Western. Back in the late 1940s when I was getting close to graduating from high school, they used to stage Saturday-night prizefights down in the Veterans Auditorium. Not boxing matches but prizefights, a name that rings in the ear something like *cockfight*. One night the two main-event fighters, always heavyweights, were some hulking Indian and a white farmer from a little dairy-farm community.

The Indian, I recall, had the word "Mother" carved on his hairless chest. Not tattooed, but carved in the flesh with a blade, so the scar tissue spelled out the word in livid welts. The white farmer looked soft and his body was alabaster, pure white, except for his wrists and neck, which were dark, burned-in-the-fields red, burnished red. While they hammered at each other we hooted from the stands like gibbons, rooting for our favorites on strictly territorial and racial grounds, and in the end were all disappointed. The white farmer went down like thunder about three times, blood snorting from his nose in a delicate spray and decorating his whiteness like in, say, the movies. The Indian simply retreated to his corner and refused to go on. It didn't make any sense.

We screeched and stomped, but the Indian just stood there looking at the bleeding white man, and the white man cleared his head and looked at the Indian, and then they both shook their heads at each other, as if acknowledging some private news they had just then learned to share. They both climbed out of the ring and together made their way up the aisle. Walked away.

Real Western. Of course, in that short-lived partnership of the downtrodden, the Indian was probably doomed to a lifetime on the lower end of the seesaw. No dairy farms in a pastoral valley, nor morning milking and school boards for him. But that is not the essential point in this equation. There is a real spiritual equivalency between Redmen and Rednecks. How sad and ironic that they tend to hit at each other for lack of a real target, acting out some tired old scenario. Both, with some justice, feel used and cheated and disenfranchised. Both want to strike back, which may be just walking away, or the bad answer, bloody noses.

☙

Nobody is claiming certain Rednecks are gorgeous about their ways of resolving the pain of their frustrations. Some of them will indeed get drunk in honky-tonks and raise hell and harass young men with long hair and golden earrings. These are the bad Rednecks.

Why bad? Because they are betraying themselves. Out-of-power groups keep fighting each other instead of what they really resent: power itself. A Redneck pounding a hippie in a dark barroom is embarrassing because we see the cowardice. What he wants to hit is a banker in broad daylight.

But things are looking up. Rednecks take drugs; hippies take jobs. And the hippie carpenters and the 250-pound, pig-tailed lumberjacks preserve their essence. They are still isolated, outrageous, lonely, proud, and mean. Any one of them might yearn for a nurse, a double-wide, a blue roan Appaloosa, and a sense of place in a country that left him behind.

☙

Like the Indian and the buffalo on the old nickel, there are two sides to American faith. But in terms of Redneck currency, they conflict. On the one side there is individualism, which in its most radical mountain-man form becomes isolation and loneliness: the standard country-and-western lament. It will lead to dying alone in your motel room: whether gored, boozed, or smacked makes little difference. On the other side there are family and community, that pastoral society of good people inhabiting the good place on earth that William Bradford and Thomas Jefferson so loved to think about.

Last winter after the snowmobile races in Seeley Lake, I had come home to stand alongside my favorite bar rail and listen to my favorite skinny Redneck barmaid turn down propositions. Did I say *home*? Anyway, standing there and feeling at home, I realized that good Redneck bars are like good hippie bars: they are community centers, like churches and pubs in the old days, and drastically unlike our singles bars where every person is so radically his or her own.

My skinny barmaid friend looked up at one lumberjack fellow, who was clomping around in his White logger boots and smiling his most winsome. She said, "You're just one of those boys with a sink full of dishes. You ain't looking for nothing but someone dumb enough to come and wash your dishes. You go home and play your radio."

A sink full of dirty dishes. And laundry. There are aspects of living alone that can be defined as going out to the JCPenney store and buying $33 worth of new shorts and socks and T-shirts because everything you own is stacked up raunchy and stinking on the far side of the bed. And going out and buying paper plates at Kmart because you're tired of eating your meals crouched over the kitchen sink. You finally learn about dirty dishes. They stay dirty. And those girls, like my skinny friend, have learned a thing or two. There are genuine offers of solace and companionship, and there are dirty dishes and nursing. And then a trailer house, and three babies in three years, diapers, and he's gone to Alaska for the big money. So back to barmaiding, this time with kids to support, babysitters.

Go home and play your radio.

There is, of course, another Montana. Consider these remarks from the journals of James and Granville Stuart, 1862:

> **January 1, 1862.** Snowed in the forenoon. Very cold in the afternoon. Raw east wind. Everybody went to grand ball given by John Grant at Grantsville and

a severe blizzard blew up and raged all night. We danced all night, no outside storm could dampen the festivities.

January 2. Still blowing a gale this morning. Forty below zero and the air is filled with driving, drifting snow. After breakfast we laid down on the floor of the several rooms, on buffalo robes that Johnny furnished, all dressed as we were and slept until about two-o'clock in the afternoon, when we arose, ate a fine dinner, then resumed dancing which we kept up with unabated pleasure . . . danced until sunrise.

January 3. The blizzard ceased about daylight, but it was very cold with about fourteen inches of snow badly drifted in places and the ground bare in spots. We estimated the cold at about thirty-five below, but fortunately there was but little wind. After breakfast all the visitors left for home, men, women, and children, all on horseback. Everyone got home without frost bites.

Sounds pretty good. But Granville Stuart got his. In the great and deadly winter of 1886–1887, before they learned the need of stacking hay for winter, when more than one million head of cattle ran the Montana ranges, he lost two-thirds of his cow herd. Carcasses piled in the coulees and fence corners come springtime as flowers grew up between the ribs of dead longhorn cattle, and the mild breezes were reeking with decay. A one-time partner of Stuart's, Conrad Kohrs, salvaged 3,000 head out of 35,000. Reports vary, but you get the sense of it.

Over across the Continental Divide to where the plains begin on the east side of the Crazy Mountains, in the Two Dot country, on bright mornings you can gaze across the enormous swale of the Musselshell, north and east to the Snowy Mountains, fifty miles distant and distinct and clear in the air as the one mountain bluebell you picked when you came out from breakfast.

But we are not talking spring, we are talking winter and haystacks. A man we know, let's call him Davis Patten, is feeding cattle. It's February, and the snow is drifting three feet deep along the fence lines, and the wind is carrying the chill factor down to about thirty below. Davis Patten is pulling his feed sled with a team of yellow Belgian geldings. For this job, it's either horses or a track-layer, like a Caterpillar D-6. The Belgians are cheaper and easier to start.

Davis kicks the last remnant of meadow hay, still greenish and smelling of dry summer, off the sled to the trailing cattle. It's three o'clock in the afternoon and already the day is settling toward dark. Sled runners creak on the frozen snow. The gray light is murky in the wind, as though inhabited, but no birds are flying anywhere. Davis Patten is sweating under his insulated coveralls, but his beard is frozen around his mouth. He heads the team toward the barns, over under the cottonwood by the creek. Light from the kitchen windows shows through the bare limbs. After he has fed the team a bait of oats, then Davis and his wife Loretta will drink coffee laced with bourbon.

Later they watch television, people laughing and joking in bright Sony color. In his bones Davis recognizes, as most of us do, that the principal supporting business of television is lies, truths that are twisted about a quarter turn. Truths that were never truths. Davis drifts off to sleep in his Barcalounger. He will wake to the white noise from a gray screen.

It is important to have a sense of all this. There are many other lives, this is just one, but none are the lives we imagine when we think of running away to territory.

Tomorrow Davis Patten will begin his day chopping ice along the creek with a splitting maul. Stock water, a daily chore. Another day with ice in his beard, sustained by memories of making slow love to Loretta under down comforters in their cold bedroom. Love, and then quickfooting it to the bathroom on the cold floors, a steaming shower. Memories of a bed that reeks a little of child making.

The rewards of the life, it is said, are spiritual, and often they are. Just standing on land you own, where you can dig any sort of hole you like, can be considered a spiritual reward, a reason for not selling out and hitting the Bahamas. But on his winter afternoons Davis Patten remembers another life. For ten years, after he broke away from Montana to the Marines, Davis hung out at the dragster tracks in the San Joaquin Valley, rebuilding engines for great, roaring, ass-busting machines. These days he sees their stripped red-and-white dragchutes flowering only on Sunday afternoons. The *Wide World of Sports*. Lost horizons. The intricate precision of cam-shaft adjustments.

In the meantime, another load of hay.

Up in towns along the highline, Browning and Harlem and Malta, people are continually dying from another kind of possibility. Another shot of Beam on the rocks and Annie Greensprings out back after the bars are closed. In Montana they used to erect little crosses along the highways wherever a fatality occurred. Awhile back, outside Browning, they got a dandy. Eleven deaths in a single car accident. *Guinness Book of World Records*. Verities. The highway department has given up the practice of erecting crosses: too many of them are dedicated to the disenfranchised.

Out south of Billings the great coalfields are being strip-mined. Possibilities. The history of Montana and the West, from the fur trade to tomorrow, is a history of colonialism, both material and cultural. Is it any wonder we are so deeply xenophobic and regard anything east of us as suspect? The money and the power always came from the East, took what it wanted, and left us, white or Indian, with our traditions dismantled and our territory filled with holes in the ground. Ever been to Butte? About half the old town was sucked into a vast open-pit mine.

Verities. The lasting thing we have learned here, if we ever learn, is to resist the beguilements of power and money. Hang on to your land. There won't be any more. Be superstitious as a Borneo tribesman. Do not let them photograph our shy, bare-breasted beauties as they wash clothes along the stream bank. Do not let them steal your soul away in pictures, because they will if they get a chance, just as Beadle's Dime and Nickel Westerns and Gene Autry B movies gnawed at the soul of this country where we all live. Verities have to be earned, and they take time in the earning—time spent gazing out over your personal wind-glazed fields of snow. Once earned, they inhabit you in complex ways you cannot name, and they cannot be given away. They can only be transmogrified—transformed into something surreal or fantastic, unreal. And ours have been, and always for the same reason: primarily the titillation of those who used to be Easterners, who are everywhere now.

These are common sentiments here in the mountain West. In 1923 Charlie Russell agreed to speak before the Great Falls Booster Club. After listening to six or seven booster speeches, he tore up his own talk and spoke. This is what he said:

> In my book a pioneer is a man who turned all the
> grass upside down, strung bob-wire over the dust
> that was left, poisoned the water and cut down the

trees, killed the Indian who owned the land, and called it progress. If I had my way, the land here would be like God made it, and none of you sons of bitches would be here at all.

So what are we left with? There was a great dream about a just and stable society, which was to be America. And there was another great dream about wilderness individuals, mountain men we have called them, who would be the natural defenders of that society. But our society is hugely corrupt, rich, and impossibly complex, and our great simple individuals can define nothing to defend, nothing to reap but the isolation implicit in their stance, nothing to gain for their strength but loneliness. The vast, sad, recurrent story that is so centrally American. Western Rednecks cherish secret remnants of those dreams and still try to live within them. No doubt a foolish enterprise.

But that's why, full of anger and a kind of releasing joy, they plunge their Snowcats around frozen lakes at ninety miles an hour, coming in for a whiskey stop with eyes glittering and icicles bright on their whiskers, and why on any summer day you can look into the sky over Missoula and see the hang-gliding daredevils circling higher than the mountains. That's why you see grown men climbing frozen waterfalls with pretty colored ropes.

And then there seems to be a shooting a week in the double-wide village. Spastic violence. You know, the husband wakes up from his drunk, lying on the kitchen floor with the light still burning, gets himself an Alka-Seltzer, stumbles into the living room, and there is Mother on the couch with half her side blown away. The 12-gauge is carefully placed back where it belongs on the rack over the breakfront. Can't tell what happened. Must have been an intruder.

Yeah, the crazy man inside us. Our friends wear Caterpillar D-9 caps when they've never pulled a friction in their lives, and Buck knives in little leather holsters on their belts, as if they might be called upon to pelt out a beaver at any moment. Or maybe just stab an empty beer can. Ah, wilderness, and suicidal nostalgia.

Which gets us to another kind of pioneer we see these days: people who come to the country with what seems to be an idea that connection with simplicities will save their lives. Which simplicities are those? The condescension implicit in the program is staggering. If you want to feel you are being taken lightly, try sitting around while someone tells you how he envies the simplicity of your life. What about Davis Patten? He says he is staying in Montana and calling it home. So am I.

Despite the old Huckleberry Finn–mountain man notion of striking out for the territory, I am going to hang on here, best I can, and nourish my own self. I know a lovely woman who lives up the road in a log house, on what is left of a hard-earned farmstead. I'm going to call and see if she's home. Maybe she'll smile and come have a glass of beer with me and my cronies.

Drinking and Driving

DEEP IN THE FAR HEART of my upbringing, a crew of us sixteen-year-old lads were driven crazy with ill-defined midsummer sadness by the damp, sour-smelling sweetness of nighttime alfalfa fields, an infinity of stars and moonglow, and no girlfriends whatsoever. Frogs croaked in the lonesome swamp.

Some miles away over Warner Range was the little ranch and lumbermill town of Lakeview, with its whorehouse district. And I had use of my father's 1949 Buick. So, another summer drive. The cathouses, out beyond the rodeo grounds, were clustered in an area called Hollywood, which seemed right. Singing cowboys were part of everything gone wrong.

We would sink our lives in cheap whiskey and the ardor of sad, expensive women. In town, we circled past the picture show and out past Hollywood, watching the town boys and their town-boy business, and we chickened out on the whores and drank more beer, then drove on through the moonlight.

Toward morning we found ourselves looping higher and higher on a two-track gravel road toward the summit of Mount Bidwell, right near the place where California and Nevada come together at the Oregon border. We topped out over a break called Fandango Pass.

The pass was named by wagon-train parties on the old Applegate cutoff to the gold country around Jacksonville. From that height they got their first glimpse of Oregon, and they camped on the summit and danced themselves some fandangos, whatever the step might be.

And we, in our ranch-boy style, did some dancing of our own. Who knows how it started, but with linked arms and hands we stumbled and skipped through the last shards of night and into the sunrise. Still drunk, I fell and bloodied my hands and stood breathing deep of the morning air and sucking at my own salty blood, shivering and pissing and watching the stunted fir and meadow aspen around me come luminous with light, and I knew our night of traveling had brought me to this happiness that would never bear talking about. No more nameless sorrow, not with these comrades, and we all knew it and remained silent.

Seventeen. I was safe forever, and I could see seventy miles out across the beauty of country where I would always live with these friends, all of it glowing with morning.

We learn it early in the West, drinking and driving, chasing away from the ticking stillness of home toward some dim aura glowing over the horizon, call it possibility or excitement. Henry James once said there are two mental states, excitement and lack of excitement, and that unfortunately excitement was more interesting than lack of excitement. Travel the highways in Montana, and you will see little white crosses along the dangerous curves, marking places where travelers have died, many of them drunk, and most of them searching and unable to name what it was they were missing at home. It's like a sport: you learn techniques.

For instance, there are three ways to go: alone, with cronies of either sex, or with someone you cherish beyond all others at that particular moment. We'll call that one love and save it for last.

Although each of these modes can get tricky, alone is the most delicate to manage. Alone can lead to loneliness, and self-pity, and paranoia, and things like that—the trip can break down into dark questing after dubious companionship.

The advantage of going it alone lies, of course, in spontaneity and freedom. You don't have to consult anybody but your inclinations. You touch that warm car, and you climb in for a moment and roll down the window, just to see what it would be like.

And then, it's magic—you're rolling, you're gone, and you're riding. Shit fire, you think, they don't need me, not today. I'm sick. This is sick leave. You know it's true. You've been sick, and this day of freedom will cure your great illness. Adios.

Say it is spring, as in *to rise or leap suddenly and swiftly,* the most dangerous and frothy season, sap rising and the wild geese honking as they fly off toward the north. "Ensnared with flowers, I fall on grass." Andrew Marvell.

It might be the first day of everything, in which we re-discover a foreverland of freedom and beauty before the invention of guilt. A day when the beasts will all lie down with one another. Hummingbirds in the purple lilac.

What we are talking about is the first day of high and classical spring here in the temperate zones: one of those pure and artless mornings somewhere toward the latter part of May or early June in the countries where I have lived when the cottonwood leaves have sprung from the bud and stand young and pale and green against the faint, elegant cleanliness of the sky. We are talking about walking outside into such a morning and breathing deeply.

Where I like to head out of Missoula is upstream along the Blackfoot River, the asphalt weaving and dipping and

the morning light lime-colored through the new leaves on
the aspen, with some fine, thin, fragile music cutting out
from the tape deck, perhaps Vivaldi concerti played on the
cello. Such music is important in the early day. It leaves a
taste as clean as the air across the mountain pastures, and it
doesn't encourage you to think. Later, there will be plenty
of thinking.

But early on all I need is the music, and the motion of
going, and some restraint. It always seems like a good idea,
those mornings up along the Blackfoot, to stop at Trixie's
Antler Inn just as the doors are being unlocked. One drink
for the road and some banter with the hippie girl tending bar.

But wrong.

After the first hesitation, more stopping at other such
establishments is inevitable. And quite enjoyable, one after
another. The Wheel Inn on the near outskirts of Lincoln,
Bowman's Corner over south of Augusta, with the front
of the Rockies rearing on the western skyline like purity
personified.

Soon that fine blue bowl of heaven and your exquisite
freedom are forgotten, and you are talking to strangers and
to yourself. No more Vivaldi. It's only noon, and you are
playing Hank Williams tapes and singing along, wondering
if you could have made it in the country-music business.
By now you are a long and dangerous way from home and
somewhat disoriented. The bartenders are studying you like
a serious problem.

You have drifted into another mythology, called lonesome traveling and lost highways, a place where you really
don't want to be on such a fine spring day. Once, it seemed
like pure release to learn that you could vote with your feet,
that you could just walk away like a movie star. Or, better yet, load your gear in some old beater pickup truck and

drive. Half an hour, the vainglorious saying went, and I can have everything on rubber. Half an hour, and I'll be rolling. You just watch, little darling.

For some of us, the consequences of such escape tended to involve sitting alone with a pint bottle of whiskey in some ancient motel room where the television doesn't work. The concept was grand and theatrical, but doing it, getting away, was oftentimes an emotional rat's nest of rootlessness. Country music, all that worn-out drifter syncopation, turned out to be another lie, a terrific sport but a real thin way of life.

☙

So, some rules for going alone: forget destinations; go where you will, always planning to stay overnight. Stop at historical markers and mull over the ironies of destiny as you drive on. By now you are listening to bluegrass, maybe a tape from a Seldom Scene concert. And you are experiencing no despair.

Think of elk in the draws, buffalo on the plains, and the complex precision of predator-prey relationships. Be interesting, and love your own company. There is no need to get drunk and kill somebody on the road. Quite soon enough it will be twilight, and you can stop in some little town, check in at one of the two motels along the river, amble down to the tavern, and make some new friends. Such a pretty life.

☙

Traveling with cronies is another matter. Some obvious organizational efforts are implicit. There stands your beloved car, warm in the sun. You touch a fender and turn away and backtrack toward your telephone, which magically starts ringing. Others have the same idea. My rig, your ice chest, bring money, we're traveling.

But the real logistical niceties lie in the chemistry of compatibility. Not just every good friend is a fit companion for the heedless expeditions of a summer drive. Each stop and turnoff must seem the result of consultation with mutual inclinations. Nothing spoils traveling more quickly than endless debate, or any debate at all. Trust the driver. Everybody knows what we're looking for. Take us there.

Which is where? Looking for what? Call it ineffable— that which cannot be expressed or described and is not to be spoken of. Traveling with cronies can't be heedless without unspoken agreement.

Back when we were young and idiotic, we would head up to the Stockman's Bar in Arlee, hit the Buffalo Park in Ravalli, move on to the 44 Bar north of St. Ignatius, and then make the Charlo turn to Tiny's. From there whim led the way until we ended up in the Eastgate Lounge in Missoula around midnight. The circuit was called The Inner Circle.

Say the afternoon sky is streaked white, and spring winds drive storm clouds over the peaks of Montana's Mission Mountains. This is the Flathead Valley, and the town is Charlo, and though it may seem impersonal now, it need not be. If you are in any way sensible, your next move should be simple and clear and rewarding. You and your companions will clump down the stairs and into Tiny's Tavern. The place used to be called Tiny's Blind Pig, *blind pig* being prohibition code for tavern. The old name, for those of us who stopped by when we were passing through, implied a connection with the romance we were seeking—an outlaw dream of prohibition, dusty black automobiles just in from a rum-run to Canada, blond gum-snapping molls. As newcomers we ached to be a part of Montana—and here it was, the real goddamned item.

One night my brother was shooting pool at Tiny's with

a wiry old man, an electrician by trade as I recall. During a lull in the bar talk I heard something that stood the hair on the back of my neck. "Son of a bitch," my brother said, "I wouldn't have to cheat to beat you."

Oh, pray for us, Lord. Outlanders in a bar filled with local ranchers and their brawny sons celebrating another victory for the best eight-man football team in the history of Montana. Do not let them beat on us—at least, not on me. Take my brother.

The rancher next to me, about a foot taller than I will ever be, looked sideways and grinned. "Don't know about you," he said, "but I ain't going over there. Them old black eyes take about three weeks to heal." By the time I had bought him and me a drink, my brother and the electrician were finishing their game without any further hint of warfare.

Well, I thought, got myself home again. Home is a notion such backcountry taverns seem to radiate—at least if they're places that longtime patrons and their barkeep hosts have imprinted with the wear and damage of their personalities. Tiny's was shaped as much as anything by the old man who owned it when I first went there—ancient and hurting, hobbling around on crutches, a former police chief from Miami, Florida, with a huge collection of memorabilia in glass cases around the bar—over 5,000 different kinds of beer bottles, intimate snapshots of Hitler taken in the 1930s, fine obsidian arrowheads, gem-quality Kennedy half-dollars. Tiny is dead now, and they've changed the sign over the doorway. But his collections are still in place.

Homes and love, if they are to exist as more than fond children of the imagination, most often take us by surprise on back roads. On my way to Missoula almost every day I pass the old Milltown Union Bar, where Dick Hugo used to do his main drinking in the days when he was serious about it. Above the doorway white heads of mountain goat and bighorn sheep, sealed in Plexiglas bubbles, contemplate those who enter. As Hugo said in a poem about the Milltown, "You were nothing going in, and now you kiss your hand." In another poem, about another barroom, Hugo named the sense of recognition and homecoming I expect upon going into one of the taverns I love. His poem begins, "Home. Home. I knew it entering."

Indeed, what are we looking for? In July of 1969 I came to Montana to stay, bearing a new Master of Fine Arts degree from the flooding heartland of Iowa. I had just finished up as a thirty-five-year-old, in-off-the-ranch graduate student in the Iowa Writers' Workshop, and I had lucked into a teaching job at the University of Montana. I was running to native cover in the West; I was a certified writer, and this was the beginning of my real life at last.

During that summer in Iowa City—drinking too much, in love with theories about heedlessness and possibility—I was trying to figure out how to inhabit my daydream. We lived in an old stone-walled house with a flooded basement out by the Coralville Reservoir, listening to cockroaches run on the nighttime linoleum and imagining Montana, where we would find a home.

Every morning the corn in the fields across the road looked to have grown six inches; every afternoon the skies turned green with tornado-warning storms; and every night lightning ran magnificent and terrible from the horizons. My wife said they ought to build a dike around the whole damned state of Iowa and turn it into a catfish preserve. The U-Haul trailer was loaded. After a last party we were history in the Midwest, gone to Montana, where we were going to glow in the dark.

The real West started at the long symbolic interstate bridge over that mainline to so many ultimately heart-breaking American versions of heaven, the Missouri River. Out in the middle of South Dakota I felt myself released into significance. It was clear I was aiming my life in the correct direction. We were headed for a town studded with abandoned tepee burners.

But more so—as we drove I imagined Lewis and Clark and Catlin and Bodmer and even Audubon up to Fort Union on the last voyage of his life in 1843, along with every wagon train, oxcart, cattle drive, and trainload of honyockers, all in pursuit of that absolute good luck that is some breathing time in a commodious place where the best that can be is right now. In the picture book of my imagination I was seeing a Montana composed of major postcards. The great river sliding by under the bridge was rich with water from the Sun River drainage, where elk and grizzly were rumored to be on the increase.

Engrossed in fantasies of traveling upriver into untouched territory, I was trying to see the world fresh, as others had seen it. On April 22, 1805, near what is now the little city of Williston in North Dakota, Meriwether Lewis wrote:

> ... immense herds of buffalo, elk, deer, and ante-
> lopes feeding in one common and boundless pasture.
> We saw a large number of beaver feeding on the
> bark of trees along the verge of the river, several
> of which we shot. Found them large and fat.

By 1832, at the confluence of the Missouri and the Yellow-stone, the painter George Catlin was already tasting ashes while trying to envision a future—just as I was trying to imagine what had been seen. Catlin wrote:

> ... the native Indian in his classic attire, galloping
> his wild horse, with sinewy bow, and shield and lance,
> amid the fleeting herds of elks and buffaloes. What

a beautiful and thrilling specimen for America to
preserve and hold up to the view of her refined
citizens and the world, in future ages! A *nation's
park*, containing man and beast, in all the wild and
freshness of their nature's beauty!

Think of Audubon responding eleven years later, on May
17, 1843, in that same upriver country around Fort Union:

Ah! Mr. Catlin, I am now sorry to see and to
read your accounts of the Indians you saw—how
very different they must have been from any that
I have seen!

On July 21, Audubon writes:

What a terrible destruction of life, as it were for
nothing, or next to it, as the tongues only were
brought in, and the flesh of these fine animals were
left to beasts and birds of prey, or to rot on the spots
where they fell. The prairies were literally covered
with the skulls of victims.

On August 5 Audubon finishes the thought:

But this cannot last; even now there is a perceptible
difference in the size of the herds, and before many
years the Buffalo, like the Great Auk, will have dis-
appeared; surely this should not be permitted.

In our summer of 1969 we poked along the edge where
the Badlands break so suddenly from the sunbaked prairies, imagining the faraway drumming of hooves, Catlin's
warriors on their decorated horses coming after us from

somewhere out of dream. Not so far south lay Wounded Knee.

We studied the stone faces of our forefathers at Mount Rushmore and didn't see a damned thing because by that time in the afternoon we were blinded by so much irony on a single day. We retired for the night to a motel somewhere south of the Devils Postpile in Wyoming. I was seeing freshly, but not always what I hoped to see. The distances were terrifying.

By the time we reached Missoula, I had disassociated my sensibilities with whiskey, which gave me the courage to march up the concrete steps to Richard Hugo's house, only a block from the Clark Fork River, where the Village Inn Motel sits these days. I rapped on his door. He studied me a moment after I introduced myself. "You're very drunk," he said.

Well hell, I thought, now you've done it.

"Wait a minute," Hugo said. "I'll join you."

Home, I thought, childlike with relief. This was the new country I had been yearning for, inhabited by this man who smiled and seemed to think I should be whatever I could manage.

I was lucky to know Dick Hugo, and his collected poems, *Making Certain It Goes On,* heads my list of good books written about the part of the world where I live. Dick loved to drive Montana; his trips were imaginative explorations into other lives as a way toward focusing on his own complexities. He made the game of seeing into art, and his poetry and life form a story that lies rock-bottom in my understanding of what art is for.

Once we drove over to fish the Jefferson River on a summer day when we were both hungover to the point of insipid visionary craziness. We didn't catch any fish, and I came home numb, simply spooked, but Dick saw some things and wrote a poem:

Silver Star

This is the final resting place of engines,
farm equipment and that rare, never more
than occasional man. Population:
17. Altitude unknown. For no
good reason you can guess, the woman
in the local store is kind. Old steam trains
have been rusting here so long, you feel
the urge to oil them, to lay new track, to start
the west again. The Jefferson
drifts by in no great hurry on its way
to wed the Madison, to be a tributary
to the ultimately dirty brown Missouri.
This town supports your need to run alone.

What if you'd lived here young, gone full of fear
to that stark brick school, the cruel teacher
supported by your guardian? Think well
of the day you ran away to Whitehall.
Think evil of the cop who found you starving
and returned you, siren open, to the house
you cannot find today. The answer comes back wrong.
There was no house. They never heard your name.

When you leave, leave in a flashy car
and wave goodbye. You are a stranger
every day. Let the engines and the farm
equipment die, and know that rivers
end and never end, lose and never lose

their famous names. What if your first girl
ended certain she was animal, barking
at the aides and licking floors? You know
you have no answers. The empty school
burns red in heavy snow.

Each time I read "Silver Star" I rediscover a story about
homes, and the courage to acknowledge such a need, a story
about Dick and his continual refinding of his own life, and
an instruction about storytelling as the art of constructing
road maps, ways home to that ultimate shelter which is the
coherent self. Montana is a landscape reeking with such
conjunction and resonance. They fill the silence.

Not long ago, on a bright spring morning, I stood on the
cliffs of the Ulm Pishkun where the Blackfeet drove dusty
hundreds of bison to fall and die. Gazing east I could dimly
see the great Anaconda Company smokestack there on
the banks of the Missouri like a finger pointing to heaven
above the old saloon-town city of Great Falls where Charlie
Russell painted and traded his pictures for whiskey—only
a little upstream from the place where Meriwether Lewis
wrote, having just finished an attempt at describing his first
sight of the falls:

> After writing this imperfect description, I again
> viewed the falls, and was so much disgusted with
> the imperfect idea it conveyed of the scene, that
> I determined to draw my pen across it and begin
> again; but then reflected that I could not perhaps
> succeed better. . . .

After so many months of precise notation, all in the
service of Thomas Jefferson's notion of the West as useful, in one of the most revealing passages written about the

American West, Lewis seems to be saying: *But this, this otherness is beyond the capture of my words, this cannot be useful, this is dream.* The dam-builders, of course, did not see it his way.

Behind me loomed the fortress of the rock-sided butte Charlie Russell painted as a backdrop to so much history, with the Rockies off beyond on the western horizon, snowy and gleaming in the morning sun. This listing could go on, but I was alone and almost frightened by so many conjunctions visible at once, and so many others right down the road: the Gates of the Mountains and Last Chance Gulch and even make-believe—Boone Caudill and Teal Eye and Dick Summers over west on the banks of the Teton River, where it cuts through the landscapes of *The Big Sky*— history evident all around and the imaginings of artists and storytellers intertwined. Charlie Russell and Bud Guthrie and Dick Hugo and Meriwether Lewis created metaphoric territory as real as any other Montana in the eye of my imagination.

We all play at transporting ourselves new into new country, seeing freshly, reorienting ourselves and our schemes within the complexities of the world. It is a powerful connection to history and the grand use we make of storytelling as we incessantly attempt to recognize that which is sacred and the point of things.

Which brings us to our most complex option, traveling with lovers. In Missoula, in the heart of winter, if you are me, you talk in a placating way to the woman you love. It is about three days after you forgot another country custom, The Valentine Party. You suggest ways of redeeming yourself. You talk to friends. An expedition forms.

This paragon of a woman owns an aging four-wheel-drive Chevrolet pickup, three-quarter-ton, and she and I and her twin boys set off in that vehicle. Only praying a little bit. Good rubber, but a clanking U-joint. The friends—a southern California surfer hooked on snow skiing of all varieties and a lady of his acquaintance—set off in that lady's vintage Volvo. We also pray for them. The Volvo wanders in its steering, in a somewhat experimental way. But no need for real fear. These are Montana highways.

Out of Missoula we caravan south through the Bitterroot Valley, where—before the subdivisions—Tom Jefferson could have seen his vision of pastoral American happiness realized. The Volvo wanders, the U-joint clanks, and we are happy. We wind up over Lost Trail Pass, where Lewis and Clark experienced such desperate vertigo in the wilderness on their way west. At the summit we turn east, toward the Big Hole Basin and a town named Wisdom. At 6,000 feet, the altitude in the Big Hole is too much for deciduous trees. The only color is the willow along the creeks, the red of dried blood.

We pass along the Big Hole Battlefield, where Chiefs Joseph and Looking Glass of the Nez Percés suffered ambush by Federal troops under General Oliver Otis Howard on the morning of August 11, 1877. Casualties: Army, 29 killed, 40 wounded; Nez Percé, by Army body count, 89 dead, most of them women and children. We are traveling through the rich history of America.

Winter has come down on this country like a hammer, but the defroster is working perfectly, and there is a bar in Wisdom with dozens of stuffed birds and animals on display around the walls. The place is crowded with weekend snowmobile fans in their bright insulated nylon coveralls. There is a stuffed quail on a stand with its head torn off. All that's left is just a little wire sticking out of its neck. What fun that night must have been.

The bar is fine. No one cares when we bring in our own cheeses and stoneground wheat crackers. We slice on the bar top, scatter crumbs. The bartender cleans up our mess. Smiles. The kids play the pinball machine all they want. We have hot drinks. So we are slightly tipsy, not to say on the verge of drunk, when we line out south toward Jackson. This is the deep countryside of Montana, and no one cares. The Volvo doesn't wander as erratically. The U-joint has made peace with itself. Which is something country people know about mechanical devices. They oftentimes heal. At least for a little while.

The Big Hole is called the "Land of 10,000 Haystacks." Nearby, a country man is feeding his cattle. Pitching hay with ice in his mustache. He has been doing it every day for two months. He has a month to go. Feeding cattle never was any fun. We do not think about such matters.

Beyond Polaris we head up a canyon between five-foot banks of snow and we are arrived. Elkhorn Hot Springs. Right away, we like it. Snowshoeing and cross-country in all directions, and for our surfer friend, a dandy little down-hill area only about three miles away. We have a cabin with a fireplace that works fine after the wood dries out. Up in the lodge they are serving family-style dinners. And cheap. You know—roast beef and meat loaf and real mashed potatoes and creamed corn and pickled beets. And on and on. Maybe this is the moment to break out the bottle of rum.

Eventually we wander down to the hot baths, the indoor sauna pools and the outdoor pool, and the snow falling into our mouths. Snowball fights in the water. Rowdiness. Young boys in swimming suits created from cutoff Levi's. And the next day, sweet red wine in the snow and white chilled wine in the evening, and the ache from all the skiing melting out of our knees into the hot water.

But electricity is in fact the way nature behaves. Nothing lasts. That was winters ago. My surfer friend went off hunting the last good wave. He wrote from Australia, extolling the virtues of the unexamined life. The Volvo is dead; the U-joint is fixed. Desire and the pursuit of the whole is called love.

How to Love This World

There is only one question:
how to love this world.

—Mary Oliver, "Spring"

THE GREAT FLOATING MOON was more silvery than white in the luminous blue of an early summer sky over the Tetons. Hung over and semi-heartbroken when I woke at sunup in Jackson, I'd gotten out of town in a hurry, before any true sense of my own isolation could come catch me.

It was a getaway that didn't work. Alongside Teton Lake, leaning against the fender of my yellow Toyota, studying the daylight moon, I was anxious and frightened to an almost breathless state. This moon was what was, and I was alone in its vicinity, under its gaze. Much as I wanted to love the silence and light, that white moon was an intimation of unfathomable dooms and infinities.

Jack Turner, a thinking man's climbing guide, tells of lying on his back on top of the highest peak in the Tetons of a morning, and seeing flashes of white, which turned out to be pelicans circling a mile above him at some great elevation, sporting in the glory of things so far as anyone could tell; one of the prime ways of curing panics that inhabit an untethered soul: playing. Maybe, without my knowing, that morning, those pelicans were up there as I shivered and hit the road for Missoula. As the Chuang-tzu put it:

> *. . . never consent to be one thing alone.*

⌒

Outside Ketchum, Idaho, a house was built to enclose a barn. There was a run-down barn in a field, and someone with endless money built a house around that barn, including it into their living room, as decor. Locals thought it was a great joke. Others moaned about outlanders and being taken over by "Hollywood."

"Those people don't live here. They're just looking for a place to hide." We all know stories like these, mirrors in which we see the foundation story behind many of the troubles we have in the West, stories having to do with insensitivity and presumed injustice. We blame the strangers. It's a way to hypnotize and paralyze ourselves.

⌒

A tall man with an orange-stained mustache said something to the effect that nobody knew how mean winter could be until they had tried the cowboy life in Montana. He told of men riding horses and motorcycles into country bars. He said anybody tough enough to survive winter in Montana was liable to do just any damned thing they could think of.

Such stories stayed with me on my first trip to Missoula, through Spokane and the Idaho Panhandle and the miners' towns like Kellogg and Wallace (the bordellos were still open in those days). I was looking for what I took to be a genuine world to inhabit. I wanted to be someone that I could understand and stand—a romantic idea that seems commonplace in the West these days. It's a story a lot of people are acting out.

Heading over Lookout Pass I studied ranch buildings in the valley below, at the edges of timber. They looked to be remnants from the sort of medieval world I'd grown up in during the slower and simpler days before World War II when country people I knew revered good horses and killed their beef at home and gathered wild greens for the table from roadsides in summer. The northern Rockies seemed like an undiscovered land, thick with secrets no one could bother to keep. A woman I know told me about growing up in a shack on the flats west of Missoula alongside the Clark Fork River, and the way her people had dynamited fish in the fall. They'd gather the killed and floating trout and suckers from a rowboat with nets, and their family would live through the winter off fish canned in glass jars. She told me this to emphasize that she was a native, and that my catch-and-release fly-fishing world could go piss up a rope so far as she was concerned, and why she wasn't thrilled when upscale Missoula restaurants began featuring fresh salmon flown in from Seattle and Alaska. She'd eaten enough fish for a lifetime. It was an honest way of speaking by a woman who valued her origins.

Sammy Thompson's Eastgate Liquor Lounge and the Trail's End Tavern in Missoula became my social centers. Sammy was a generous man who grew up tending bars in the railroad, ranch-hand taverns along Woody Street in Missoula (they were gone when I got to town); he was a stockcar-racing, speedboat man. Showing off for a woman, running his boat hard under stars over Flathead Lake, Sam hit a drifting log and flipped. They clung to that floating speedboat until sunup. Then Sam, a skinny fellow, no meat on his bones, slid underneath. His funeral wasn't anything I wanted to know about. I felt as if someone had torn up the dance floor. Maybe the man in the moon.

But springtime alleyways were thick with blossoming clumps of purple and white lilac and people on their way to work stopped on the street to spend time talking to the mayor (they still do). We left our doors unlocked. "Them locks," somebody told me, "only keep out honest people."

So I didn't entirely despair; I tried to discover reasons for taking care, that discovering another common concern in the West these days.

☞

One way of enlarging ourselves involves the educational comedy of hitting the road, sometimes called "The Traveling Cure," which has been a communal enterprise in the West since the fur trappers and the wagon trains, like Huck Finn gone to territory, Hemingway in Spain and Africa, Willie Nelson and cowboy beatniks heading down their lonesome highways. Such goings can be understood as ways of seeking the freedom to be whatever you can manage.

North of Missoula, where Highway 93 crests along the southern boundary of the National Buffalo Range, you are witness to the vast weave of rock walls that are the Mission Mountains hanging like a curtain on the eastern horizon. In October, the mountains are dusted with snow while hayfields in the valley below remain green even if the willows and cottonwood along Post Creek are turning red. That's how it was when I saw it in 1969, my first autumn in Montana. I thought of it as a paradise where a man might make a life if he had any sense.

But the Flathead Valley hasn't quite been a white man's paradise for the taking. It's the heart of the 1.25 million acre Flathead Indian Reservation, governed by the Confederated Salish and Kootenai Tribes, a sovereign nation inside the United States. History has been ferociously sad and unjust for Native American people, but on the Flathead Reservation the tribes are taking charge of their future with what looks to be a good ration of fairness, common sense, and restraint.

On Good Friday a gang of us visited the brick cathedral in the reservation town of St. Ignatius, at the foot of the Missions. Native people chanted the liturgy in Salish and carried a wooden approximation of Christ around to outdoor fires marking the Stations of the Cross. We didn't believe in their prayers; we wondered if they did; and we stopped going, maybe because we were unsettled by the fact that we saw our religious situation reflected in the mirror of theirs.

Jim Crumley leased a cabin near Polebridge, just across the North Fork of the Flathead River from Glacier Park. Jim was working on a novel, but often he was on his motorcycle, into the curves, he said, and he had company. In June we drove the Going-to-the-Sun Highway across the mountainous spine of Glacier just before it was closed by a summer snowstorm.

The interior of Glacier is an empire of crystalline lakes beneath knife-edged precipitous cirque walls of rock carved over millennia by glaciers, of hanging ice fields and waterfalls and dark gorges cut by rushing waters. On that afternoon in June, reefs of misty clouds hung below us against the evergreen slopes. Our chatter turned silent. The honking world had been transformed by natural and evolving beauties; it had gone distant from anything we ordinarily experienced. Yet it was absolutely recognizable, if forgotten and intricate. It was as if we were recalling a place where we played as children.

Later that summer we walked in. In scrubby timber off the trail to Bowman's Lake, flecked with shadows and sunlight, I stepped from one to another platter-shaped and luridly colored mushroom, crushing them. It was like walking on stones across water. Then I killed a grouse with a stone's throw (we cooked it primitively, impaled on a green branch along with trout). That night we got stoned, having traded part of our catch to some fellows down the lake who'd forgotten their food but remembered to bring a grocery sack stuffed with smoking materials, and we sipped shots from one of our bottles of whiskey and talked about the chance of venturing into willows along the creek, in search of trout but encountering a grizzly. We were at least aware enough to wonder if this was the way Hemingway thought—the short happy life—and laughed and laughed and laughed. Later I woke to behold moonlight in a wash across the stillness of the lake. What if this, I thought, was the last thing you ever saw? In the morning we stayed out of the willows, trolling open water along the edge of the lake from a makeshift raft held together by baling wire and an old pair of suspenders.

On a warm summer night a few years later, Mary Pat Mahoney was dragged from a campground tent in a Glacier Park; she was killed and partially eaten. She was a friend, but I was consumed with anger more than sorrow and wondered why. I would wake in the night and think of revenge. And I was finally moved to write a story called "We Are Not in This Together." Before the writing was done I had to admit that the best revenge was going on with your days— peacefulness while pursuing your own chances. There's a Native American Bear Mother story in which a woman is stolen away from her people to live with a bear. She gives birth to twins who are half human and half bear. The Bear Husband is killed by the woman's brothers, but her sons, because they are willing to recognize the sacredness of bears, become great hunters. The moral complexities of that story are a way traditional people acknowledge kinship with animals, which are often thought of as making us the gift of their lives so that we may survive. It is a story of death and renewal, vanishing and coming back from a winter of hibernation (enactments of sacred return may have been the earliest religious story), and of our irrevocable connection to the interwoven rhythms of nature.

Stories hold us together, in ourselves, and with one another. We use them to reimagine ourselves, the most necessary art. In the Bob Marshall Wilderness with Annick Smith I stood beside horses amid plumes of bear grass below a high rocky escarpment along the Continental Divide that is called the Chinese Wall. Our guide told of rutting elk sounding off for one another in autumn, when the larch have turned golden and their needles have fallen. Experts say there are more elk up there than when Lewis and Clark made their way along the Missouri, just east, in 1805. We vowed to return, not to hunt, intent on being witness, but we've never gone again. The possibility is like money in the bank.

Annick and I walked in four or five miles to Wall Lake in British Columbia, just out of Waterton Park, at the foot of a curving, vertical wall of stone with midsummer ice at the top. The next morning we saw a wolverine—a creature that's been almost exterminated from the tame world. It resembled a reddish dark badger, implacable, untamable, and almost feverish in the quick absolute way it foraged on a gravel bar near the water. It was there, then aware of us, and gone. I never expect to see another wolverine. That encounter will have to stay with me, and I hope it will; it was good for my soul to encounter a creature so unavailable to our agendas, to see that such a way of going at life was still possible.

Memories move in our brains like small fires, electricity that in fact flows through us, like blood. We are inescapably part of every lighting storm, mushroom, and bear, grizzly or not, wedded as can be, like trout in the stream of what is.

⁓

It was a tradition. On Sunday mornings in mid-June, wild roses blooming along the fence lines through the meadows, we'd drive upstream along the Big Blackfoot River (which was not the river filmed in *A River Runs Through It,* even though it's the river in which Norman Maclean's brother Paul did his magical fishing). East beyond the Continental Divide we were into the rolling glaciated country along the Rockies Front, short-grass prairies reaching east for a thousand miles.

We were heading for the rodeo in the village of Augusta, among cottonwood along the Sun River. We drank in the darkness of taverns, walked three or four hundred yards through light and shadows under the trees to the rodeo, in the sunlight, while country music played on the public-address system. Men and women unloaded roping horses from aluminum trailers, and we ate hot dogs and bought beer to load our cooler and made our way to seats near the chutes, where the bellowing and stink and cursing and laughter and flying mud and snot and the odor of piss were thick around us. World-class riders landed airplanes out in the meadows, came out of the chutes on their bucking horses or bulls, then flew off to make some other show that night, maybe the one in Cody, Wyoming. We took to it like a day at the circus.

The old ways become picturesque and commoditized. Bull riders and team ropers and cowboy poets are understood as entertainers just as we were taken to be tourists, with pockets full of money, willing to buy, but at the same time seriously condescending to the locals. All around, it's a recipe for misunderstanding that colors a lot of transactions in the West.

What many of us were looking for, as I understood it, is connection to the resolute life before the invention of incessant irony. A friend called it, "the real world, an actual time." Before, perhaps, our affairs went virtual. But rodeo is not a good place to look. The cowhand world, when it goes public, despite bloody noses, is pretty much a media invention—the sort of thing we so often see—glitz and images. "The bigger the hat," a bowlegged fellow said to me, grinning and shaking his head and spitting snoose, "the smaller the ranch."

The way I like to travel these days is through distance and its towns with no destination. Richard Hugo, a survivor of multiple dislocations who helped many of us in the West define our lives, was the poet laureate of such going. Dick came from Seattle at the age of forty to teach at the University of Montana. After his wife left, Dick was alone, as he understood it, with too much time on his hands and with his automobiles, Buick convertibles, in which he would run the territories with the top down on sunny days, good jazz on the radio, looking for a town where he could spend an evening in the tavern talking to strangers, hoping for thoughts that would trigger a poem. The last stanza of his "Driving Montana" is one of our defining texts in the northern Rockies:

> Tomorrow will open again, the sky wide
> as the mouth of a wild girl, friable
> clouds you lose yourself to. You are lost
> in miles of land without people, without
> one fear of being found. . . .

North of Augusta, at a property owned by the Nature Conservancy, a wildlands fen just below the Rockies Front where the grizzlies still come out on the plains as they did before the white men came, at a place called the Pine Butte Swamp, local people held a gathering in honor of the novelist Bud Guthrie in October of 1993. Bud was very old, clearly dying. He was a man who devoted much of his last energies to the preservation of what remnants of the natural world remained in the country where he had mostly lived. Men and women Guthrie had lived among for decades spoke quietly to the particularities of their friendships, and then we drove out along the Teton River, into country Bud wrote about, in *The Big Sky,* as a ruined paradise. In 1830, an old trapper in that book says, "Gone, by God, and naught to care savin' some of us who seen 'er new."

"God, she was purty onc't," that man said. It still is. We didn't know what we had missed. Perhaps the country is tracked and roaded, but it was not, so far as we could see, entirely spoiled. Bud's storytelling helped us see it not as ruined but layered with histories. Stories helped us understand what had happened in that long Montana valley where the October snow blows down from the mountains through the twilight, and stories helped us live with fragilities as we watched Bud and his friends take stock and breathe the joys of fellowship for close to the last time in the Choteau country that afternoon. We understood that our turn was coming, sooner than might be hoped, and that we ought to prepare, if such preparations are possible.

Exactly like history, stories accumulate and drive us toward being what we are. In places they come together and congregate, for instance at the Great Falls of the Missouri, seventy some miles east of the Rockies Front, where the river drops over a series of shelves, flowing out onto the plains. The Missouri was the interior waterway to the West, as much a northwest passage as existed, a route of travel that connected the northern Rockies to St. Louis, New Orleans, the Atlantic, and civilizations like France and England.

On June 13, 1805, Meriwether Lewis sat by the falls and wrote that they were "the grandest sight I ever beheld." A grizzly chased Lewis into the river the next day, and the expedition spent a month making an 18-mile portage around the falls in country thick with prickly pear cactus, but danger and difficulties were not the message. The journals kept by Lewis and Clark are among our defining documents in America, like *Leaves of Grass* and Lincoln's address at Gettysburg. They tell us to go toward possibility.

Upstream from the falls, in the 1880s, a visionary named Paris Gibson laid out a community he called Great Falls. He planted thousands of oak and elm trees on avenues staked across the prairies and hired men to go out at dawn and water them from wagonloads of barrels filled out of the Missouri. Charlie Russell set up his log-cabin studio on one of those avenues. These days it's a district of aging rich-man houses shaded by those enormous trees.

In 1887 the Great Northern Railroad arrived; Black Eagle, the first of four hydroelectric dams situated at the falls, was completed in 1891; the Anaconda Company began setting up their first copper-reduction plant shortly thereafter. Great Falls is a place where western economic dreams worked out, at least for a while.

I stood atop the Ulm Pishkun, a cliff just north of the Missouri, a dozen miles west of Great Falls, where native tribesmen once drove stampeding bison to their death (it was a way of hunting). The abandoned brick smokestack over the old Anaconda Company refinery towered into a clear morning. Off west I could see snowy peaks of the "shining mountains" on the Rockies Front, looking just as they did when Lewis and Clark saw them. Here, I thought, a history of dreams in this part of the world. But not all of that story, not by a long shot.

The dryland-farming country that locals call the "Golden Triangle," strips of fallow ground and wheat that run over the plains to the horizon, and on, begins north of Great Falls. Distances between the towns clustered at the foot of towering grain elevators on the "highline" along the Great Northern tracks were dictated by concerns about getting crops to market. This is the land of windbreaks beside white-painted farmsteads, enormous four-wheel-drive diesel tractors and millionaires with cash-flow problems (a viable wheat farm on the plains is worth a million anyway). On the plains we find ourselves wondering about the rewards of freedom that led people to stick it out through the blistering summers and blizzard winters, raising children on places where the nearest doctor was maybe fifty snow-drifted miles away—for details read Judy Blunt's *Breaking Clean.* The isolation is hardest to deal with, even for today's people, who can afford all the electronic connection to reality there is. Sometimes you need to get on into downtown, in person.

In Richard Ford's story "Communist," a young man, recalling an afternoon spent hunting geese on one of the lakes that fill depressions left by glaciers, says, ". . . I looked toward the Highwood Mountains twenty miles away, half in snow and half dark blue at the bottom. I could see the little town of Floweree then, looking shabby and dimly lighted in the distance. A red bar sign shone. A car moved slowly away from the scattered buildings."

He hears geese on the lake, thousands, before he sees them, a clamoring ". . . that made your chest rise and your shoulders tighten with expectancy. It was a sound that made you feel separate from it and everything else, as if you were of no importance in the grand scheme of things."

That feeling of separation can overwhelm you. Life often seems to go on in ways not connected to the doings of the so-called "Great World." Ambitious young people leave early and never go home for more than a few days at Christmas. Many of the people who stay develop a deep mistrust of anything beyond their emotional horizon. It is a way of being dysfunctional.

James Welch was a Blackfeet/Gros Ventre writer who

did some of his growing up near the Milk River beyond Harlem. In his first novel, *Winter in the Blood,* he took on those feelings and showed us a young man finding his way beyond them into the rhythms involved in connecting to his people and himself amid such distances. It is a supremely *useful* book for people in the northern West—both Native Americans and whites. Any life, anywhere we see, can be rewarding, if we allow, if we have imagination enough.

"Some people," the young man says in *Winter in the Blood,* "will never know how pleasant it is to be distant in a clean rain, the driving rain of a summer storm. It's not like you'd expect, nothing like you'd expect." Maybe it's all in learning to see the splendor of what is, what you have.

Wallace Stegner spent his boyhood in the Cypress Hills on the border between Montana and Saskatchewan. In *The Big Rock Candy Mountain* he writes, "They could stand quietly in the door and watch the good rain come, the front of it like a wall and the wind ahead of it stirring up dust, until it reached them and drenched the bare packed earth of the yard, and the ground smoked under its feet, and darkened, and ran with little streams. . . ." The good rain: a reason for loving this world. On those plains, so many miles east of the shining mountains, we are in what can be thought of as "The Land of Little Kingdoms," with nothing but territory between them—Hutterite colonies, and cowboy towns like Miles City, and homesteader towns like Ryegate. You can drive from Ryegate to the Snowy Mountains, windy country where a settlement boom came before World War I, and pass abandoned homesteads, one after another. Houses and barns lean with the wind, shingles blown away. This is the land of ICBM silos. This country has been talked about as "Buffalo Commons," a preserve devoted to biodiversity if not for the few endlessly stubborn settlers who remain.

After driving those prairies for hours, Annick and I

walked into a motel in Jordan, Montana, a town of about 600 souls south of the reservoir backed up behind the Fort Peck Dam. "Are you," the clerk asked, "paleontologists?" Jordan, it turns out, is where bone hunters headquarter when they're searching clay-bank-badlands washes above the Missouri for another skeleton of *Tyrannosaurus rex*. Out there we are continually reminded of infinities.

Militia crusaders, some years back, holed up in the vicinity of Jordan. Locals wished they'd go away, but tolerated them. Settlers on the plains have a long history of political extremism. No one gets too excited so long as there's no serious trouble. Radicalism in that part of the world started with the Nonpartisan League in North Dakota—farmers calling for state-owned banks and grain elevators. In 1918 the Nonpartisan League set up a newspaper called *Producers News* in Plentywood, in the northeastern corner of Montana. After 1920 many of the maybe 3,000 voters in Sheridan County were Communists; they ran the county for a few years. By 1930 about 500 citizens were still voting the straight Communist Party ticket. It was another attempt at organizing an economic and spiritual kingdom: where enterprises attempted to create a man-made paradise on earth, a try at making the world go your way—one of our oldest, most honorable traditions in America.

But maybe the plains were already a paradise. We see movie herds of bison running in the otherwise sappy *Dances with Wolves,* and can't articulate reasons why we are so moved. By the 1890s the buffalo were mostly gone from the plains. The Crow warrior Two Leggings said, "Nothing happened after that. We just lived. . . . There is nothing more to tell."

To try understanding what it was like to come upriver on the Missouri in the 1830s and 1840s, study the art of George Catlin and Karl Bodmer, who were there, and look into Catlin journals and Audubon's *Missouri River Journals.* Read contemporary accounts in Ian Frazier's *Great Plains* and Merrill Gilfillan's *Magpie Rising* and Barry Lopez's *Winter Count.* If you should go there in the summertime, driving west through bright fields of sunflowers in North Dakota, travel with those books and go slow. You will find yourself in touch with glories that can break your heart; loss, as we know, is always part of love.

⁂

The story of John Colter's several hundred mile wintertime walk into the environs of Yellowstone is one more of our defining legends in the West. The autumn and winter of 1807–08, through country no known white man had yet seen, Colter went from Fort Lisa, at the junction of the Big Horn River and the Yellowstone, down to Jackson Hole and the far side of the Tetons, and back through what would be Yellowstone Park. I want to think he was running on wisdom, and not simple courage; I want to think his isolation was something he accepted as a version of what we always have. I like to think Colter loved his chance to be where he was. Yellowstone in winter, seven thousand seven hundred feet in elevation at the lake, where the nighttime lows are thirty and forty below, the snows a dozen feet in depth, and the hot sulfur springs boil up, the grass still green beside them, down in a warm enclosure with drifted snowbanks rising high above your head. Think of spring, bison wandering through the mist near the steaming river where the trumpeter swans glide on glassy ponds. Colter had been with Lewis and Clark as they climbed the long grade to Lemhi Pass, on the Continental Divide, imagining that the beginnings of the great River Columbia, an easy route to the Pacific, might lie just on the other side. Instead they saw the long run of blue mountains across what is now central Idaho, range after range. John Colter knew there was no easy way out. I like to think he might have studied a full daylight moon over the Tetons, as I did a hundred and eighty years later, and felt he was as close to the sweet center of things as he would ever need to be, and thus privileged.

White People in Paradise

One: Aristocracy

> *If heartaches were commercials,*
> *we'd all be on TV.*
>
> —John Prine

MY FATHER IS ALIVE in my imagination. I wouldn't
be surprised to see him at the rail in some Montana
tavern, eyeing me with his old irony, tapping his Shriner's
money clip on the bar while a tattooed bartender pours his
drink. The drive from Oregon wore him out the last summer he came to Montana. He was eighty-seven and going
on nine heart attacks. "The next one," he said, "and I'm out
of lives, like a house cat." He drank scotch and milk for
angina. And we traveled from barroom to barroom in the
Bitterroot Valley, which once could be thought of as a kind
of out-West Shangri-La, a happy kingdom surrounded by
wilderness mountains. We stopped on a bridge over the
Bitterroot and watched yellow rafts coming at us, fishermen flashing fly lines in the sun. My father spoke to nobody. "They'll never see it."

Partly, I understood, he was talking about the way the
world was disappearing. He was talking about the luck of
his life and what had come of it. In his thirties he had the
good fortune to control a huge untouched farming property

in southeastern Oregon, a marshland of peat soils that had been building over thousands of years—the kind of place that does not much exist anymore. He got his hands on a paradise of waterbirds and fertility, and he remade it into what he understood as useful, a sprawling system of irrigation and drainage canals and agribusiness fields where undulating drill-rows might run straight for a mile, and he went at it with great energy, building hundreds of redwood headgates that would never rot. He brought in Caterpillar tractors and ran them day and night. People said he was crazy; he was rewarded with legendary crops. He made a lot of money on oats during World War II; he bought racehorses and a Beechcraft Bonanza. Actors and politicians showed up for the hunting (a quarter million ducks and geese migrated through the valley each year). He bought shotgun shells and Usher's Scotch by the pickup load. But the governor of Oregon died when the Bonanza went down in the November twilight of 1943; the peat blew and burned and went saline; birds started frequenting some other flyway. After we sold out in 1967, my father retired to the Oregon coast. He fished for salmon and smoked his pipe and kept an eye on the tides.

That moment in the Bitterroot was as close as he ever came to talking politics with me. His opinions had gone angry in old age; it was clear he despised my liberal sentiments. He was talking of the Bitterroot Valley as clear evidence of loss. Black cattle grazed belly-deep in meadows by the river, and Rain-Bird sprinklers threw rainbows over the alfalfa lands. Much of it still looks like a dream of farmboy heaven direct from some Thomas Jefferson Book of the Sacred. "They turned it into another goddamned trailer park," my father said. The roadsides were built up with shops and parlors—beauty and auto, plumbing, welding, fencing, chain saw, and ranchette realtor and recreational vehicle, taxidermy, and so on to the end of human need. It was not anybody's idea of how things ought to be. My father was talking about the West when it was in a condition I would never see.

He was talking about a past that looked—at least to him—more valuable than any foreseeable future. He was saying something about regret, telling himself he was ready to die. Or maybe he was done telling himself. Maybe he was telling me. He died in May of 1990; the tenth heart attack got him. This is where I have to be careful. I want to honor my father and his anger. He was descended from people who took what they wanted and understood themselves as a natural ruling class. They were absolutely sure that they deserved what they got; they worked for it; they sacrificed and cared for themselves and their people; and they were pitiless in their ability to despise weakness in strangers. I wonder what my father saw in his most secret sight of the right life. It's my guess he wanted to live out his life surrounded by friends and children and fertile fields of his own designing. I think he wanted to die believing he had been in on the creation of a good sweet place. Those pilgrims believed stories in which the West was a promise, a faraway place where decent people could escape from the wreckage of the old world and start over. Come to me, the dream whispers, and you can have one more chance.

We like to claim the West is a place where you can have a shot at being what you want to be. You can come to terms with yourself. Freedom, in a livable community, is supposed to be the point of things. It's our primary mythology, and it sort of works out, more so if you're white and have some money. Men like my father, and the women who shared their ambitions, were our aristocracy. They are mostly dead. The West they left us is partway ruined; many of our enterprises are a considerable distance out on the rocks; and many of us are somewhat bewildered and heartbroken. We learned to name ourselves in what we took to be the nobility of their story. But they left us a society that's semi-functional at best. Up the Clark Fork River from the place where I live in Missoula, the Milltown Dam is to be torn out because it holds behind it six and a half tons of sediment thick with toxic materials from the mining days in Butte. Our mountains erode under clear-cut logging; our farm towns are dying; we suffer the whims of a boom-or-bust economy, a history of semi-genocidal racism, and a good-old-boys class system (we love to imagine we are enormously independent and egalitarian, yet so many of us are powerless in any operative sense). And we're always broke.

But we still listen to old promises in the wind. This time, we think, we'll get it right. We'd better. Like a house cat, like my father, the West has only got so many lives.

Two: Farming in the Free World

> *And time has whittled down the cabbage*
> *leaves to thin white wings.*
>
> —Brian Patten, "Through the
> Tall Grass in Your Head"

I've spent mornings fishing in streams along the White River Syncline in the Bob Marshall Wilderness, and in the afternoons stood looking down on the wilderness elk pastures along the Sun River from the escarpment of the Chinese Wall. We search for mushrooms under cottonwood along sandbars by the Clark Fork River, play golf in the afternoon, go sit on a terrace overlooking the lights of Missoula while we get into grapefruit juice and Herradura, and sleep at home with the door unlocked. People ask why

I live in Montana. I give them answers like that. They're kind of true.

Montana has been called a small town with long streets (real long, 600 miles from the Idaho border to the conjunction of the Missouri and the Yellowstone). A friend who lives across the Continental Divide told of falling in with "psychic spooks" while driving the prairies for days. "It doesn't do much for my religious situation," he said, "but it's so beautiful I kind of forget."

That's what we like to think we're doing here, enjoying the solace of connection to consequential and even reassuring infinities. But the infinities can be too infinite. Radical freedom can be translated into utter isolation. Crossing the Rockies at Marias Pass, beside the Northern Pacific tracks along the southern edge of Glacier Park, in October, while it was spitting snow, I saw a moose come to the edge of the asphalt and gallop away; it was swift, huge-headed, and spooky like a horse. I was dropping toward East Glacier, where generations of tourists got off Pullman cars to be greeted by Blackfeet Indians wearing authentic beadwork costumes. Beyond were the windblown reservation towns where Blackfeet people actually live, and east of them lay the dryland-farming country known as the "Golden Triangle"— alternate strips of crop and fallow ground. Winter wheat, planted in the fall, sprouts, lies dormant through the cold months, and starts growing again in the spring. Harvested in midsummer, it is a primary dollar crop in Montana (in 1924 the northeastern Montana town of Scobey was the largest wheat-loading center in North America).

Out on those farmer plains we are in the land of ICBM silos and blizzards, shimmering summertime, tight white-painted farmsteads, elaborate windbreak tree lines, and millionaires (a viable wheat farm is worth at least a million). It can be understood as a land of monocultures, both agricultural and spiritual. Cut Bank, Shelby, Chester, Kremlin, Havre, Chinook, Harlem, Malta, Wolf Point, Poplar: the towns string along south of the Canadian border on a route called "the highline." Distances between them are dictated by concerns about getting crops to the railroad. Their names embody a pattern of ethnic settlement like a teaching poem about the mix of culture that once was, or might have been: Native American, German-Russian, Dutch, Mediterranean, wolf-hunter.

East of Malta, in the twilight, I saw what looked to be a boy and a girl, one long-haired and the other not, with wind-burned faces; they were skinny ranch kids in their after-school clothes, carrying damp burlap sacks to cover the late crops against frost in the night. I recall my own childhood, my father's garden, and the stinking burlap. I had sulked during those hours covering cucumbers; darkness came down, bearing the cold. I wondered if those children outside Malta felt as distant as I had. Maybe their feelings of insignificance are even more overpowering; I didn't grow up with television and the sight of taillights feathering away into the darkness.

Three: History in Heaven

> *. . . the party killed 3 beaver and a deer.*
> *We can send out at any time and obtain*
> *whatever species of meat the country af-*
> *fords in as large a quantity as we wish.*
>
> —Meriwether Lewis

On the 8th of May, 1805, William Clark climbed a rise on the north side of the Missouri River. The country, back toward the Dakotas, in the words of Meriwether Lewis, was "level and beautiful on both sides of the river, with large herds of buffalo distributed throughout."

From where Clark stood, above the highway, I could see bottomland farms (no wolves, no buffalo, nothing wild but varmints and waterfowl and occasional chaos in the soul). Upstream lay the intricately eroded territory of the Missouri badlands, the country of white cliffs, where the Missouri and its tributaries cut a complex watershed through the highlands plateau. Sunlight reflected off the quarter-million-acre lake (134 miles long, 1,520 miles of shoreline) backed up by the largest earth-filled structure on the planet (126 million cubic yards), the Fort Peck Dam.

William Clark, if he'd seen such waters, might have thought they were an arm of some undiscovered ocean. In the Cambrian period, 570 million years Before Present, waters covered the plains. As they rose and fell over the millennia an explosion of multicellular life died and was buried under the mudflats. Examples are preserved in Burgess Shale found high in the Canadian Rockies, north of Banff, a town where the citizens put up street signs in both English and Japanese (for Pacific Rim tourists).

Five hundred or so million years later (seventy million years Before Present), in the Cretaceous Period, another sea washed beaches of the plains country in the Age of Dinosaurs. The Rockies were rising, and the dinosaurs migrated to nest on high ground along the Rockies Front (eggs have been found, with baby duckbills inside, just east of Choteau, Montana).

In 1902 an expedition from the American Museum of Natural History, led by a man named Barnum Brown, went to Montana and found, in the Hell Creek sandstone formation in the Missouri River badlands, something nobody had ever seen—the remains of the carnivorous *Tyrannosaurus rex,* the terrible-toothed 40-foot, 8-ton comic-book "King of the tyrant lizards." Of four resurrected *Tyrannosaurus* skeletons on display in American museums, all were found in Garfield County, Montana, a fact that generates great local pride.

The five-turbine powerhouse/surge tower at the Fort Peck dam is a structure of such 1930s monumental scale it might be imagined as a lost remnant of some heroic civilization (maybe it is). In the museum at the base there is a huge three-horned skull of a *Triceratops*. Just beyond through soundproof windows, in a metallic powerhouse-control room, a man sat watching banks of motionless dials. It was the perfect metaphor—our interwoven biological past sealed off from the unshadowed future.

Four: A Future Like the Past

> *Paradise lies all around.*
> *Can you not see it?*
>
> —Gnostic parable

Jordan, Montana, is frighteningly isolated by any down-town standard; they have a hospital, but the nearest doctor is ninety miles away in Miles City. The woman at the motel asked if I was a paleontologist. That night in the Hell Creek Bar a handsome woman asked me to dance with her to the jukebox, but I wouldn't. Nobody else was dancing, and I was in the presence of ranchland people: quiet men; Indian women keeping their own company; an overdressed court-ing couple trying it out in public; three midcareer gents wearing expensive boots (cow buyers or bankers or govern-ment employees who were talking a lot); a lank teenaged boy in tennis shoes who was watching his father as his father drank. There was a time when I belonged in places like that, but I quit country life and the ranch business, and I was sure those people could spot me for a defector. I wanted to sulk in the corner and keep quiet like a spy.

I'd come to Jordan with the notion of finding out what the locals thought about the "Buffalo Commons." What that amounts to is this: across the northern short-grass plains in eastern Montana, adjacent to the Missouri River badlands, there is an enormous expanse (15,000 square miles) of sparsely populated prairie where a multitude of birds and other species survive. It's argued that this "Big Open" constitutes a national treasure and might be turned into a wildlife preserve, where antelope, deer, elk, and buffalo (and wolves and grizzly bears) could roam as they once did, biodiversity enshrined. Citizens there, especially in the little towns, could make a living off hunters and the tourist trade (or, some call it, the servant business).

A hundred and fifty years ago millions of bison roamed the North American prairies. The last wild ones were shot out south of Jordan in 1886, by William Hornaday, a taxidermist, for the Smithsonian. Hornaday sent twenty-four hides, sixteen skeletons, and fifty-one skulls back to Washington, D.C. It was his nineteenth-century way of preserving the buffalo. Frank and Deborah Popper proposed to restore them. Sociologists at Rutgers, they did a lot of homework in the plains states between the 98th meridian and the Rocky Mountains, seeking what they called "distressed areas," counties "that had lost at least 50 percent of their population since 1930. An over-10-percent loss between 1980 amd 1988. Four or fewer people per square mile. High median age. Twenty percent or more in poverty."

A lot of counties qualified. The Poppers said such areas should not have been settled in the first place. They proposed a 139,000 square-mile national grasslands that would include a lot of the western Dakotas, western Nebraska, eastern Montana, and areas in Kansas, Oklahoma, Texas, Colorado, New Mexico, and Wyoming. They proposed tearing down the fences. This is nightmare talk to long-time inhabitants of the short-grass plains, an old story. In his 1878 report for the United States Geologic Survey, John Wesley Powell said the short-grass plains could never support intensive cropping because of inadequate rainfall and recurrent drought. His report was ignored. By 1910 James Hill had built his Great Northern Railroad across the Montana highline. He was trying to sell tickets, claiming 320 acres would support a homestead farm; settlers came to the plains bearing possessions; it was a migration. They built shacks, they tried to farm, most failed, most left after having wasted years in dirt-eating poverty. Many citizens of Jordan are descendants of those who stayed. They think of themselves as the survivors. Now they find people talking about turning their homeland into a preserve for wild beasts; some are understandably angry and humiliated. They think outsiders value the buffalo more than they value the sacrifices of their people.

Imagine telling people in Jordan that you think the Buffalo Commons is the seed of a necessary idea. It is our duty, I would tell them, as the dominant species, to preserve tracts of land in its native condition. Biological interactions necessary to ensure life in its continuities are astonishingly complex and cannot take place in islands of semi-wilderness like national parks.

Imagine saying, "We're taking your land, we're kicking you out, we're sorry, but our purposes are larger than yours." I imagine telling them we need to replant the world; I imagine talking about the mental health of our species. It is good for our sanity to witness nature at its most multitudinous; such encounters function in our imaginations as a sight of possibility—dinosaurs and on to multiplicities, life everlasting. I imagine telling those people that we continue to inhabit an age of sacred beasts, as we destroy them.

No doubt I would be dismissed as another nitwit, a missionary come to take everything their people had suffered for. It's easy, amid distances on the short-grass plains, as in eastern Montana, where the rhythms of life don't much change for generations, to find you are estranged from national moods. The people in Jordan have good reason to go xenophobic. They don't fear strangers so much as deplore them. Talking about the Buffalo Commons might be a good way to get your ass kicked in a place like the Hell Creek Bar in Jordan, Montana. Or not. Maybe those good people would tell me paradise is all around. Maybe they would tell me to take a walk out into the world and take a look. I did, next morning. I saw a broom-tailed red fox on the outskirts of Jordan. A great blue heron flew under the highway bridge and came out on the other side.

Five: Going for the Sand

> *The essential American soul is hard,
> isolate, stoic, and a killer.*
>
> —D. H. Lawrence

In the fur-trapper days, it is said, Indian women were so incessantly raped by white men that they resorted to a strategy called "going for the sand." When trappers showed up those women would go to the creeks and pack their vaginas with sand.

In January of 1870, the temperature forty below, Major Eugene Baker and his Second U.S. Cavalry massacred a band of Blackfeet-Piegan camped on the Marias River. Their lodges were overrun with smallpox victims (it was rumored traders deliberately gave them the disease with infected blankets). One hundred and seventy-three Indians died; the survivors agreed to settle on the reservation.

James Welch, the Blackfeet writer, told of searching out the Marias massacre site while doing research for his masterpiece, *Fools Crow,* a novel in which the Marias massacre is the pivotal event. The site wasn't marked, he said, it was just an open field by the river. The Custer Battlefield is, on the other hand, a National Monument; we celebrate history in disingenuous ways. Welch said he drove on, from Montana into Canada, to the sacred sand hills of the Blackfeet (they were covered with dune-buggy tracks). "They believed you would go live in the sand hills after you died. It would be much like your present life, traveling with your people, and hunting."

The Blackfeet, it seems, believed they lived someplace close to heaven already. They believed life was supposed to be the way it already was. But, in the terrible winter of 1883–84, the Blackfeet were abandoned by their federal agent, left without food, too weak to hunt. Rescue missions found the living mad with hunger and grief and wolves, inside their lodges, tearing at the flesh of the unburied. Six hundred had starved to death—a quarter of the tribe.

Economic development comes hard on isolated reservations like that of the Blackfeet. On a snowy morning in Browning I saw a knot of men shuffling and blowing their noses as they told jokes in the parking lot in front of a liquor store while waiting for the doors to open. So many wake up drunk so much of the time; fetal alcohol syndrome is an ongoing urgent-health problem on reservations all over the West. In 1985, on the Wind River Reservation of Wyoming (Arapahoe and Shoshone, population somewhere near 5,000), a series of 9 young men, ages 14 to 25, killed themselves. Scott Swistowicz, a teacher at St. Stephen's Indian School, said, "I think the futility of what they saw in their futures became overwhelming." Wind River people responded by staging healing ceremonies. They began re-learning their traditional languages, getting in closer touch with the old culture. It's a tough climb. The situation is roughly like that of inner-city residents; there's no work and little chance to enter a society as essentially heartless as ours. Eleven organized Indian tribes live in Montana; we have seven reservations. There is not much in the way of a ladder to climb. It is utterly necessary, in Montana and all over the West, if we want to admire ourselves and proceed into the future with some belief in our power to heal our society, that we start paying our debts to them. We must encourage native cultures as they seek to honor their own communities and help them build economies that are centered in their own cultures, completely theirs. We don't so much need a war on drugs and alcohol in America, as we need a war on anomie and powerlessness.

It is the work of national leaders to bring us to confrontation against our own coldheartedness. That they have not done so is a major political failure. Essentially leaderless, we learn to forget our dream of a just society. By embracing selfishness, we ultimately learn to despise ourselves; it could be the death of our society.

Six: Inexhaustable Riches

> *"Stranger, you're driving your ducks to a mighty poor pond."*
>
> —Overheard in the Eastgate Liquor Lounge

I stopped off the interstate in the deep-shaft mining town of Wallace, Idaho (at that time the only stoplight on I–90 between Boston and Seattle). The elegant old hotel barroom was empty except for a heavy-shouldered man down the line a couple of stools; he was drunk; his legs had been amputated above the knee. "What I got for it," he said, "was notched."

He had to be talking about a lifetime given to the mines; he was furious; he grasped the bar with his huge broken-fingered hands, lifted himself, and came after me like a crab, suspended on terrible, quivering forearms, tattoos knotting, his anger so justifiable and futile.

Butte was the Empire City of western mining. For decades Butte was the largest, richest city between Denver and the coast. Butte was whores, gambling, and knockabout violence; Butte was also families, ethnic neigborhoods, and fraternal societies. Butte was the Anaconda Copper Company, the monopoly that effectively ran Montana at its pleasure into the sixth decade of this century. Copper ore was reduced in open-hearth smelters over wood and charcoal fires; the city lived under toxic yellow smoke. Sulfuric acid dripped from the walls in 2,700 miles of tunneling, burned clothes and flesh; silicosis was epidemic. "Copper Kings" battled for possession of Butte, then sold it out in 1906, to eastern interests.

On June 8, 1917, a carbide lamp ignited a fire at the 2,400-foot level; the shaft formed a roaring downdraft chimney: this was the Speculator Mine Disaster in which 164 miners died. Three days later miners and smelter men organized the Metal Mine Workers' Union. On June 29, 1917, 15,000 men in Butte, Anaconda, and Great Falls went on strike. On the night of August 17, 1917, IWW organizer Frank Little was dragged four miles down the railroad track to a trestle and hanged by "parties unknown." A message was pinned to his shirt: "Others take notice. First and last warning." By midwinter the strike was over; the company won. In 1920 company guards fired into workers in Anaconda (one died). By 1921 Butte had been under martial law six times.

In 1955 open-pit mining began. By the time it was abandoned, the Berkeley Pit had 2,500 miles of road, it was 1,500 feet deep and had swallowed three square miles, edging toward the heart of the city. In 1968 1,700 miners lost their jobs after a 9-month strike. In 1981 the Anaconda Company was bought by the Atlantic Richfield Company (ARCO). On April 23, 1982, ARCO stopped pumping; the Berkeley Pit began filling with water rich in lead, arsenic, manganese, copper, cadmium, zinc, and sulfates at the rate of about 2½ feet per month. Those contaminants seep into the Butte water supply, and the Clark Fork River, which flows past Missoula to the Columbia and Portland and the Pacific. The scenario holds for deep mines abandoned everywhere in the Rockies: pumping stops, the water rises, contamination works its ways into streams that flow down to rivers, which flow down to cities. Nobody knows what to do.

Some of us used to celebrate St. Patrick's Day in Butte, before we got too old and fragile. We would spend the night before St. Paddy's Day in the Helsinki Bar up near the edge of the Berkeley Pit in what was left of Finntown. The next morning we'd go to the M&M Bar to start the day with a green beer served by a waitress with green hair and eye shadow. The joint was thick with men and women who had long ago decided to gamble their lives on the fate of the working class. "Let's toast the company," one of them said. We bought shots of Irish, held them to the light; his fingers were thick with broken calluses. "Fuck the company," he shouted, and we tossed them back. He cackled with happiness.

The tough, as we know, move on. "Butte," the writer Thomas McGuane told me, "can be thought of as the vibe center of Montana. The people in Butte were entitled to a great sense of defeat. They respond with humor and imagination.

It is our best model in Montana, if we want to enjoy the future at all." He's right.

When ARCO closed the mines, Butte was dying. Business and labor people got together and agreed to sit on ancient hatreds. They moved beyond lamentation and nostalgia to participate in the international network of technologies that is inevitably part of our future. And they did it as a community. It's no accident our most creative and humane politicians, Mike Mansfield and Pat Williams, came out of a town as streetwise as Butte.

Seven: Multiple Use

> *"I mean, what the hell, she's ruined anyhow."*
>
> —Overheard in the Laundromat

The West is a double-hearted dreamland: both a home in paradise and a wide-open situation where you could maybe make a killing. For so many of us, it's a difficult place to work for a living. "You can't eat the view." It's a thing people say as they justify the ongoing exploitation of our resources.

Miles City evolved into the key nineteenth-century cow town on the northern plains. You catch a sense of that glory in the Montana Bar: a stamped-tin ceiling, hand-laid Italian tile, mounted heads of a red-haired longhorn and a buffalo looking down, and in the front window, a full-mounted Audubon's bighorn sheep.

The first Audubon's bighorn was sighted on April 29, 1805, near what is now Culberston, Montana, by Joseph Field of the Lewis and Clark expedition; the last one was killed on Seven Blackfoot Creek in the Missouri Breaks in April 1916. Dinosaurs, buffalo, grizzlies, the old-growth forests—it's a story telling us we inhabit a dying place. It becomes an excuse for giving in to selfishness (most of us don't listen when somebody says the Indians were living right in the first place, in communal cultures and a sustaining relationship with the potentialities of their homeland).

Our foundation stories, from *The Big Sky* and *Shane* to *The Wild Bunch*, *Chinatown*, and *Melvin and Howard*, have always swung on the subject of easy money. Just like so many real western adventures.

I visited fourth-generation eastern Montana rancher Wally McRae at his place on Rosebud Creek, where Custer passed by on his way to oblivion at the Little Big Horn, and found McRae furious with the business community in Miles City. "They're embarrassed," he said, "by their cowboy heritage. They want big business. They want to import garbage from the East." It's true; the idea has been seriously proposed; and regional landfills will likely come into being while coal trains go east, and hazardous waste comes west by the trainload from various seaports. Montana is desperate for trade, and there's lots of open space.

McRae is something of a media figure (a cowboy poet, a 1989 winner of a National Folklife Award), but in many ways he is like my father, an innovator and traditionalist; he collects old-time photographs and tack; there are sheds filled with retired horse-drawn equipment. When I visited, McRae was dusty and tired from a morning spent getting his horses ready to take over to the Tongue River country where his roundup would begin; his wife Ruth served us a lunch of roast beef and mashed potatoes and corn and home-baked cherry pie; these are people who live close up to their source of income. McRae's home is about ten air miles downwind from the huge open-pit mines and coal-fired electrical generating plants around an energy town called Colstrip. Miles of hilly grassland have been dug up by the great shovels; conveyor belts cross horizons like something out of a sci-fi dream. The perfect air is contaminated by sulfur dioxide and nitrogen dioxide (acid rain) and carbon dioxide (think, global warming). Colstrip drove McRae and other farmers and ranchers, in 1972, to form the Northern Plains Resource Council, a populist movement that is the strongest environmental force in eastern Montana. They often stand against what is called progress (and jobs). In backland Montana that is understood as a radical position. What they really are is conservative. In such unlikely alliances, between environmentalists and traditionalists like McRae, we begin to see the politics of our future in the West. Most of us were brought up to believe the gifts of the world are to be used, but many of our ranchers and loggers, mill workers and miners are changing their minds. They are tired of seeing the mines and prairies and timber bought up by corporations and harvested for the enrichment of shareholders who live elsewhere. Never mind that they and people like them did the hands-on open-pit mining and timber-falling and cowboying; they are shamed by clear-cut timberland and saline seepage in wheat fields, plow grounds gone to dust, silted, ruined trout streams. They have been rode hard, as the saying goes, and hung up wet.

But, a new economy is likely to be a long time coming; lots of Montana people are still eager to sell their heritage. Just east of the Rockies Front, near the white-man's community of Choteau (population 1,798), over a couple of hills from that outcropping where paleontologists found fossilized dinosaur eggs with baby duckbills inside, the Nature Conservancy owns an 18,000-acre tract called the Pine Butte Swamp Preserve, a last place where grizzlies come down off the Rockies onto the plains (where they lived before we drove them to the mountains). The centerpiece in the preserve is a 2,000-acre peat land known as a fen (swamp, except that the water percolates through on its way to other lives). The fen is an intensely interwoven community of life (15 threatened species); it is at the spiritual and biological heart of a mixture of private and public lands along a 100-mile reach of the Rockies Front, which is one of the largest recovering-game ranges in the world.

Development in the Rockies Front is on hold at the moment. Environmentalists have traditionally wanted the Rockies Front declared a wilderness; oil corporations have wanted it opened to petroleum drilling in which case it wouldn't be wilderness, it would be developed. Pine Butte Swamp would be isolated from the Front. Grizzlies would stop coming from the mountains to the fen, and one more biological community would have been irrevocably frac-tured. Which would be fine with many people in Choteau; grizzlies kill cattle. And besides, think of the oil drilling. "The tax dollars. We could build a new library." It's difficult to sympathize with them. Choteau looks to be as well off as anybody in rural Montana. Their eagerness to develop the wild country seems to be driven by greed. You have to won-der if they really want the whole boomtown package: oil-field roughnecks with thousands of bucks a month in their pockets, and the fine good times, cocaine, and overloaded sewage systems and schools. You wonder if the folks in Choteau have consulted with old-timers around Evanston, Wyoming, or Wamsutter. The oil patch boomed down there about 1980. It lasted three years. They're still getting over it.

But we're petroleum junkies in America. Our enthusi-asm for energy independence may still play into the hands of the oil companies (you have to think that was always the idea). The Rockies Front may still become another national sacrifice area. We've had the beaver trade and the buffalo hunters, the gold and silver and copper mines, the home-steaders, boom times in lumber and petroleum, and each time we've ended up busted and looking for another way home. Our economy is based on a nineteenth-century public-land policy called "multiple use" (subsidizing timber, grazing, minerals, free recreational access; it was a policy designed to encourage settlement and development). And it's worked out, obviously, to be a sweet deal for the home folks and an endless windfall for timber and mining corporations. Let's hope that public indignation may someday drive a national legislative agenda to restrict commercial uses of public land, which should be thought of as a national treasure (not treasure-house). It's an idea that connects to yearnings all over our nation. Once again, the West might be understood as a last chance.

Eight: Wise Use

> *The principle supporting business now is rage.*
>
> —Richard Hugo, "Degrees of Gray in Phillipsburg"

The economic hot spots in the West are Reno (gambling), Las Vegas (gambling and defense), Salt Lake City (hi-tech industry), Boise (computers), Aspen, Jackson Hole, and Santa Fe (amenities and recreation). Hi-tech and tourism are in the saddle. They're going to be. The hordes of educated techies and tourists come mainly for some version of wildness and tend to despise the look of logging and mining (missile silos are below ground).

The list of cures for western economic problems is as long as your leg: hi-tech, low-impact manufacturing and distribution, gambling (high-rise casinos along Flathead Lake?), bilingual expeditions into the wilderness, hunting enclaves for semi-African safaris, helicopter skiing, and golf resorts; filmmakers and writers and stockbrokers with their modems hooked up to New York and Los Angeles.

It's easy to understand why many working-class people hate a future in which they see themselves for the most part excluded (except in subservient roles as hunting guides and motel maids). In old photographs we see sixty-seven loggers on the fresh-cut stump of a single ancient cedar tree. With their long saws crossed, their sleeves rolled up, they stared into the camera like kings of the forest. They knew themselves in their work, but their work is vanishing. So far they have mostly stayed at their jobs and labored as colonials at what they love and know how to do. But they tell their kids to get educated and get out; their time is ending. Our paradise is played out. The old order in the West is right to fear the environmentalists; they are going to prevail; they represent the will of the nation (except maybe in the matter of drilling for petroleum); they have a crisis on their side, and the votes; they don't care much about loggers, farmers, and miners (or economies like those in Montana and Wyoming), but they do care about what's left of the world, which they understand as invaluable and somehow to be preserved.

Nine: Putting an End to Anger

> *You just want to live in your own*
> *private Idaho.*
>
> —The B-52's

> *You take romance, I'll take Jell-O.*
>
> —Ella Fitzgerald, improvising
> on "A Fine Romance"

The quintessential nineteenth-century Montana cowboy, Teddy Blue Abbott, once told Charlie Russell that he wished he had been born a hundred years earlier, as a Sioux Indian. "They been living in heaven for a thousand years," Russell answered, "and we took it away from 'em for forty dollars a month." You can catch sadness unto death, and tire of white-man dreams, and think you want to be an Indian. It might be a way of leaving your troubles behind, vanishing into some never-never land. Or not. Even an old double-hearted trickster like Charlie Russell flirted with the idea. It is a way of saying the best that can be is come and gone. Heroes inside mountain-man fantasies of their own invention parade our streets in buckskins and beads. The West has always been a shelter for crazies drawn by our open spaces and mythology of freedom. They think anything goes. Our history can be thought of as a series of resettlements. Bonanza times are mostly over, but the dream of a good place endures. Outsiders come seeking knowable communities and a natural world in some semblance of a healthy state. Many buy their way in, fleeing urban setups that are becoming increasingly uninhabitable, however privileged. Maybe they feel some actual thing is missing from their lives and come searching for it in the West. In any event, Montana is becoming an out-West theme park. Our situation is rapidly going zoo-like. Distances are swarming with people, and the chances of silence while osprey plunge after kokanee by the Bird Islands on Flathead Lake are virtually gone. Bicoastal entertainers buy our prairies and say locals can't go hunting there anymore. Blame the rich strangers. It is a way of paralyzing ourselves.

One warm afternoon in October I walked under western red cedar in a remnant of Pacific maritime forest in western Montana. Tamarack were dropping their golden needles on the mountains and cottonwood were blooming vivid yellow along the Bull River. I used to hate people who want to harvest one of the main reasons we have for living here (call it beauty) and could not stop myself; I despised my anger. It was an indulgence, foolishness. We must learn to step on our anger. Controversies over economic fairness and class resonate throughout history. Much of any human story, of course, concerns the ongoing battle between the working stiffs and the rich and privileged. If we're going to quit reliving that story we have to talk things out and search for accord, however difficult and long-winded the undertaking. We need to see that adversarial, winner-take-all, showdown political decision-making is a way we defeat ourselves. The future starts when we begin honoring the dreams of our enemies while staying true to our own. We need to tell ourselves stories in which our society sees the devastation of the natural world as a sure way of killing each other. Institutionalizing social and economic injustice is a way of doing the same thing. Communality and mutual responsibility are fundamental. We need to acknowledge that our populations are stunningly various, with enormously diverse ideas and dreams about the future. We need to name those dreams and fold them one by one into our agendas. It's reasonable to expect politicians to take the lead in such processes, but they don't. They don't seem capable. We have to take politics back from the lawyers and the boys with money. If we can work our way through to a public consensus, lawmakers and bureaucrats will follow. Then, in Montana, we might be able to decide which coalfields to dig up and sell, what price we want for our coal if we want to sell, which is timberland and which is wilderness, and where grizzlies should live, and wolves, the buffalo and the elk (if we want them at all). We need to find money to care for our poor and our disoriented and our disabled and our dispossessed (including Native Americans, however extensive their reservations), the money to repair bridges and highways, and most fundamentally, we have to decide how to pay first-string teachers in first-rate schools (any culture's main economic hope in any long run). People came to the West and found a secure life and saw their values written into law, over generations. My grandfather and father found an untouched place. They got the first shot at it; and they inherited an old story. Take charge and make it pay. Our problems are more complex. We're responsible for imagining our way into a just society and an economy based on labor and inventiveness, rather than deep plowing in the pastures of heaven.

Lost Cowboys
(but not forgotten)

W E ARE, most of us, ethnologists in our own house and working to locate ourselves amid the clutter. Many of us consciously work to remake ourselves in the image of some long-ago land where people were healed to their lives. But, even though we have to think people have always been aware of their awareness, we also have to think they have usually tried to avoid acknowledging how much everything, including ourselves, is on-the-spot invention and make-believe.

☞

When I came to Montana I was always tracking. But, drifting through taverns like an anthropologist, I didn't know what animal I was after. I believed my life and the lives of people I knew were of little significance because we lived in an insulated city of middle-class affiliations. Lives of consequence, I thought, were being lived down the road among the drunks and Indians and working stiffs (as in, "Their lives are more *real*"; it was as condescending as could be). Like a lot of people I imagined life in its most significant cadences was taking place somewhere on our political peripheries. I was after that occasional tavern that becomes a hideout for radical funniness and the juxtaposition of dissimilar elements. A life in taverns can be like art, I thought: it can help us see freshly, our sacred duty. Humiliation and sentimental nostalgia were dominant in the cowhand music I listened to as the days drifted away. But I wasn't responsible; I was invisible, artistic, and close to paralyzed by my disengagements.

◌

First you find a metaphor like the "lost wax process" in bronze casting (the idea of a residual metallic shell around a core that has melted and drained away, i.e., cowboys in image instead of actuality), and then you name your manifestation of that metaphor (something like "Lost Cowboys"). You construct your entire piece of writing to fit the name. It's one way of trying to make sure your piece is reasonably coherent, and that it has a title you can live with.

◌

There are at least four wonderful memoirs about life on the plains: *Goodbye to a River* by John Graves, *Old Jules* by Mari Sandoz, *Wolf Willow* by Wallace Stegner, and *We Pointed Them North* by Teddy Blue Abbott and Helena Huntington Smith.

The last time Teddy Blue ever saw Calamity Jane was in Gilt Edge, Montana, just up from the Judith Basin. "I joked her about her trip and asked her: 'How'd you like it when they sent you east to get reformed and civilized?' Her eyes filled with tears. She said: 'Blue, why don't the sons of bitches leave me alone and let me go to hell my own route?'"

When Teddy Blue talked, it was always about cowboying. The later stuff was only life. "I started young and I am seventy-eight. Only a few of us are left now, and they are scattered from Texas to Canada."

"Such is life," Teddy said, "in the Far West."

∞

Sliced apples and pears, various cheeses, and very good wine—a crowd of us was whooping it up at a well-lighted reception in the Charlie Russell Museum as evening came down over the tree-lined boulevards on the north side of Great Falls. A raggedy man came in off the street. His shoes were wrapped with silver duct tape. Somebody told him the spread was free. The man smiled and poured for himself. Somebody wanted to show him out, but nobody did. I remember his judicious expression as he sipped his wine and studied a Russell painting. Uneasiness floated in that hall milling with the enfranchised, we the people with OK automobiles and new shirts, and didn't soften until it was said that he was the only person in the place Charlie Russell could have tolerated.

∞

I remember daybreak on the deserts of eastern Oregon and my father and other men who are dead now easing into a round willow-walled corral where sixty or so spooky young geldings were circling counterclockwise around the rock-solid juniper center post. My father would flip his raw-hide riata in an effortless way and drop the loop over the head of a roping horse, a quick stocking-footed bay, and I would watch as he eased down the taut rope toward the trembling animal. You see men like him in the Salt Lake City airport surrounded by businessmen wearing polished snakeskin boots and skiers bound for the mountains with peacock feathers tucked into their hatbands. Not long ago

I saw Wilfred Brimley in the Delta concourse at the Salt Lake City airport. He was backed against a wall, studying the crowd (there, I thought, the first time I saw him on a movie screen, so actual amid the silliness of *The Electric Cowboy,* there they got one of the real ones). Another lank broke-up buckaroo made his way past, limping and walking sideways like a crab, paying us no attention. It's my illusion that those old farts learned rules in a rigorous school not many of us try anymore. They know their time is over, and hate it, as anybody would, as my father did; they see us as imitation and pitiful in our dislocations. But Wilfred Brimley has become a movie star. I think of him as the first Old Postmodern Cowhand Fart, trapped in our zoo, keeper and kept. I wish I knew what he thinks.

☙

My father believed each of his wives was as good and capable as a human could be, and yet he was willing to say no woman should ever be elected to political office. "They're not fit for it," he would say. He despised the unemployed on principle, for their weakness, but he was legendary for his generosity. Men who worked for him stayed on for years. He loaned them money, bought them whiskey, hired them back, but never imagined they were his equals. The list of things my father came to despise started somewhere in the neighborhood of people who overwork the goodwill of others. The motto of the country where I come from in southeastern Oregon might be, "Take care of your own goddamned self."

☙

Snow skittered across the highway at Lost Trail Pass in early November. I was backtracking Lewis and Clark south across the Bitterroot Mountains between Montana and Idaho. What I was seeking, in my lonely-boy state of mind, with Elvis plugged into the tape deck, was a cure for my dislocations and another growing season.

It's a dis-ease that can overcome you with the first evidence of winter in the northern Rockies, when the world seems entirely distant from hummingbirds in the blooming lilacs. I'm aging, and people I know every so often die of afflictions that strike the aged; I learn to accommodate the notion that closure, as in story endings, has to do with what people we are. It was evening as I drove up along the Salmon River into canyons that rise toward the Stanley Basin. It's a drive people from Montana seem to try every so often, seeking relief from their cherished isolation and heading south toward what we understand as heedlessness in Sun Valley, or gambling in Reno and on to the alien blooming richness of the Sonoran deserts in early spring.

A friend says it's been years since he found dead, spawned-out salmon on gravel bars along the Salmon River. I grieve for those fish, and for the sad terrible grizzly bears. Grizzlies, in this part of the world, were easy to kill. There was no need to go search them out in the bushwhack mountains. A hunter could just sight in his high-velocity rifle and wait for the salmon to run. The grizzly would come to fish, and you could sit three hundred yards away with a scope and kill them like pests. I pray that deep in these mountains there are grizzlies living an invulnerable life in a paradise of their own discovering, where we will never go.

In wintertime moonlight, the icy Sawtooth Range was aglow under a swirling sky. I contemplated the serious, classical, fool-making mysteries. How to proceed? Can it be true we suffer a nostalgia for which there is no remedy on earth?

On another trip I imagined that the morning light breaking through the great windows in the Sun Valley Lodge was shattered glass. It should have been the sweetest of times, mayflies hovering in golden light under shimmering birch, the waters mysterious with evening-time trout, and nights of ease and merriment among the winsome, perfectly enfranchised folk who inhabit the Wood River Valley. I bribed the chamber-maid for a look at the third-floor room where Hemingway is reputed to have written *For Whom the Bell Tolls.* It overlooked a year-round ice rink made famous by Sonja Henie in the 1930s Ice Capades. What I saw was intimacy with the kind of frac-turing that drove Hemingway to his shotgun. *Many must have it.* I stood on a balcony, listening to birds. Their calling sang of dislocation. So I eased myself downstairs. A western film conference was underway: actors, old-time directors, schol-ars, stars like Harry Dean Stanton, Struther Martin, Buster Crabbe. I was there to learn something about the dominant mythology of my homeland. That afternoon only a half-dozen meditative souls inhabited the bar. I found myself in conversation with legendary men: the Native American actor Iron Eyes Cody and Colonel Tim McCoy of the Wyoming National Guard and MGM. As youngsters they had gone to Hollywood from the Thermopolis country in Wyoming and been stars. Now they were bemoaning modernist inauthen-ticity, as old men will. Don't mistake me; I respected them. Tim McCoy was one of the seven great stars at MGM before the invention of sound (McCoy, John Gilbert, Lon Chaney, Ramon Novarro, Buster Keaton, Marion Davies, and Lillian Gish). It was perfect: there we were, remnants, me and those once-upon-a-time moving-picture stars. Then a green-eyed handsome man moved in, wearing an orange jogging outfit, deck shoes, no socks, and a Rolex watch. He eyed us like a hired pathologist. "What you need," he said to me, "is a line." As in, we all thought, and we were right, cocaine. As in, I think now, politics, line of work, and intention. Colonel Tim McCoy froze. Iron Eyes Cody looked away in sorrow. But it was true; I needed to be tethered. I smiled, and there I was, in complicity with the green-eyed guy, cut off from those old men and what I saw as a chance at the right relationship and true reverence. But the cocaine was also a try at connection. Perhaps we are all after it.

❦

In Ketchum, over breakfast, a friend told of traveling to Santa Barbara four days a month to train as a lay analyst. Our talk led to notions of *familia,* the Latin word that unites home and family in a narrative in which we go on "making story," the most important thing we do, constantly reciting to ourselves the story that is our life. When we lose the plot, we lose track of ourselves. This is called "Narrative Dysfunction." It is no fun.

The stories we invent to live by can be marvelously wrongheaded even though we use them as teaching stories. The people inventing these stories, any of us, are often wounded and frightened by the loneliness inherent in our lives, and our stories can encourage deep selfishness. Many of us head out to the hills. "To hell with public responsibilities." Maybe, we whisper, we can find a hideout where water from a hot spring showers from a cliff above a wilderness river. We talk of nature as a resort, a place in which we might find refuge. We are talking about privilege.

❦

> . . . the road took us to the most distant
> fountain of waters of the mighty Missouri
> in surch of which we had spent so many
> toilsome days and wristless nights.
>
> —Meriwether Lewis

In motel rooms, I replayed the video of Elvis singing "You Ain't Nothing But a Hound Dog" to a real dog on the *Steve Allen Show* in 1956. Meditating on Elvis's last sad rewards

got me to Meriwether Lewis, and the high hopes that surrounded our beginnings in the West.

On Monday, August 12, 1805, Lewis was laboring uphill, heading west to the Continental Divide. Earlier in the
afternoon a man named McNeal "... exhultingly stood
with a foot on each side of this little rivulet and thanked
his god that he had lived to bestride the mighty & hereto-
fore deemed endless Missouri." Lewis "... proceeded to the
top of the dividing ridge from which I discovered immence
ranges of high mountains still to the West of us with their
tops partially covered with snow."

It was an instant of metaphoric importance. The Corps
of Discovery had been moving upriver from St. Louis for
two days short of fifteen months, since the 14th of May, 1804.
One of the objectives assigned by President Jefferson was the
discovery of an overland route for transcontinental trade and
traffic. And now, at last, men from the United States were
at the great watershed. Lewis was expecting to gaze down
on the River Columbia, a free-flowing highway that would
carry them to the Pacific in ease. What he saw was timbered
ridge after ridge, some snow-covered, feathering off to a sky
more infinite with possibility than anyone had hoped.

Lewis and Clark returned to the East and told Jefferson
that the way to the west lay over a 300-mile maze of mountains, 60 of which were covered with perpetual snows. Their
message was taken to heart. The federal government didn't
venture into the Northern Rockies again until the Stevens
railroad survey of 1855. The run of mountains was left as an
enclave to be inhabited by the Indians and the trappers and
the prospectors and bypassed by civilization and civic order.
Part of that vast enclave remains, as wilderness. It is important to our sense of Americans as a people willing to preserve that which is natural in our lives, if only by accident.

The West may be thought of as states on the cusp. If our political boundaries had been laid out by a sensible formula, Montana and Wyoming and Idaho wouldn't exist at all. Almost a hundred years ago, in his *Report on the Lands of the Arid Region of the United States,* John Wesley Powell pointed out that the natural political empathies in the West lay within the major watersheds. By cutting the West up along boundaries determined by the grid survey, which didn't reflect anything real, Powell said we were forcing our populations into artificial alliances: a telling and accurate insight to which nobody gave much attention. As a result, our states are conglomerations of unlikely allies and irresolvable dislocations. Montana, Wyoming: What's in a name? Ezra Pound pointed out that nouns name nothing real; nothing is static; verbs and process are real. In the act of naming we are constantly involved in transmogrification, making unreal.

A friend, something of a poetic fop, stopped in a tavern in Hailey, where Ezra was born, and asked if anybody had any idea who Pound might be. The barkeep, some kind of logging-camp Wobbly nihilist, grinned and recited:

> Learn of the green world what can be thy place
> In scaled invention or true artistry
> Pull down thy vanity

That's the story. Point is, I believe it. My friend says he fled up the road, to his own kind and happy hour at the Sun Valley Lodge.

In Boise, a woman named Nancy Stringfellow spent her life assembling one of the finest bookstores between Chicago and the West Coast. She wrote, "We came here in 1914, when I was four years old. Oh, it's changed since I was a girl, but there are still little towns a girl wants to get away from and a woman wants to get back to."

In May 1980, Annick Smith and I were driving home along the upper reaches of the Lochsa River, and we elected to bide and ease the miseries of travel in the undeveloped wilderness, an area called Jerry Johnson Hot Springs. We counted our blessings. The steaming creek-side pools were deserted.

We noticed a speckling of gray-white residue accumulating on the rocks. It seemed to be falling from the sky. Have you ever been back in the western wilds and imagined the technocratic world has ended? Maybe it was nukes at last, and we were the saving remnant, alive there where hot water bubbled at the edge of a snowmelt creek coming down from the western slopes of the Bitterroots. Maybe we were the last uncontaminated people on earth. But, no. It was Mount St. Helens. We were not alone. Up there in the Bitterroots, mellowing out in other hideaway hot springs, there were many like us, seeking connection to something we couldn't name that nevertheless seemed actual. Gary Snyder has said, "And that's the real work: to make the world real as it is and find ourselves real as we are within it." By which he seems to mean that it's hard to believe that we're real. We despair over children from inner-city enclaves who have been witness to too much moral chaos. For them, ideas of justice seem to be one contrivance after another, and they come to believe that the consequences of their actions are perfectly arbitrary. Lightness of being can indeed be unbearable. And it's not just an affliction of the ghettos; it's uptown and everywhere. Those of us who can, flee; we seek out the hot springs. We try to be at ease and accept the grace we find. But it seems unearned, and we are tempted to despise ourselves, even while we cultivate our decencies. Maybe our getaway was too easy. Maybe we were too willing to collapse into connection with things we claim to love, like creek-bed stones.

Mount St. Helens counted as a small apocalypse in our part of the world. That first evening, driving into Missoula from Jerry Johnson Hot Springs, the arc lights cast an orangey shimmering aura through the volcanic ash that was settling in small drifts along the streets. We seized the chance to join a long rolling knot of a party that lasted the three or four days until the rains came.

Some of us followed the action, resort to resort, Sun Valley, Boulder, Telluride, Sedona, Santa Fe, Moab, wondering where next? And some of us ended up two-hearted as we could be, understanding that life breaks easily, and meanwhile thinking about reconnecting to the rhythms of place and family. God knows some problems were left blowing in the wind, like what about everybody else, the people we've all seen, who couldn't afford the trip? There is a story about Paris, Gertrude Stein and Picasso and Matisse, and a migration of their followers to the West, in search of a union between the aesthetic and the practical, a healing connection to the natural world. This happened in Jackson Hole in the 1920s. The Modernist Rich fell for the Cowboys' native work-oriented sense of style (Oscar Wilde said the miners in Leadville were more interesting than anyone else he encountered in America because of their floppy hats and great ground-sweeping coats) but failed to understand that Cowboys and Loggers and Miners are Rednecks at heart.

Rednecks, as they are mostly understood in the West, tend to be working-class white folks whose people have been in the country for a couple of generations. They can't be defined by class or by where they grew up or by their profession. Some are timber-fallers, others are dentists. If one characteristic defines Redneck, it is, I think, a deep sense of disenfranchisement—they feel, quite justifiably, cut off from the sources of power in their culture.

At first the Modernist Rich were driven to overdress as Dudes or pseudo-Cowboys; but then they realized the actual Cowboys despised them, and besides, the Cowboys were deeply involved in unsound grazing practices that sped the destruction of the very nature that had proven to be so healing. An unsettling realization, it soon led to betrayal. The Rich reverted to Ruling-Class instincts and bought up the surrounding lands. They become Dude Ranchers and part-time Conservationists, and everything was saved except for the Cowboys.

☙

We operate in systems of metaphor that are used to define the world (both natural and social). Sad thing—we must always remodel our metaphors (models) because each always fails (not complex enough).

Artists in the American West (as everywhere), from Timothy Sullivan and Charlie Russell to the people who half buried those nose-down Cadillacs in the New Mexican desert, work toward helping us in that process of revision by inciting us to witness a version of each moment with the blinders off. It's what artists are for; they help us *see*; they drive society through the process of coming to fresh recognitions; it is a political responsibility.

☙

At midmorning in the valley where the Madison River flows through southwestern Montana, the light was absolute, as it would be in paradise if I could imagine such a place. Shadows cast by the Madison Range receded across the sagebrush foothills; a country man was baling with his New Holland hay-baler.

A Montana highway patrolman smiled when I asked about the road to the Earth First! encampment. "Newspaper?" he said. I was an aging citizen, summer haircut, in a rented Toyota. Maybe I was FBI. "No," I said. I was in fact looking for Dave Foreman, the main spokesperson for Earth First! FBI agents had gone to his house in Tucson, showed .357 magnum pistols, and dragged him to jail wearing nothing but his shorts and handcuffs. Now he was out on bail, awaiting trial, formally charged with *Conspiracy to sabotage a nuclear facility and destruction of an energy facility.* As I understood the story, it was a morality play—a good man brought down by his own heedlessness. The charismatic leader, when I found him, was retired from charisma; he had never believed in charisma; he thought charismatic leaders were a step toward fascism, always had. He despised them.

There's a story about Wovoka, a Shoshone whose visions inspired the Ghost Dance Rebellion, the spiritual movement that swept across the West like a great wind and culminated in the massacre at Wounded Knee, in December of 1890. Later, a group of plains Indians traveled horseback over great distances to consult with Wovoka at Walker Lake in Nevada. His wife came to the door of his ranchhand house. "The Messiah is tired," she said, "and wishes you would all go home."

My dealings with Dave Foreman had gone like that. Parked by the road was a Volkswagen van with Texas plates and a bumper sticker that read, *Succeed: Get the US out of Texas.* The hippie-looking driver and his friends were stopped and talking to four flat-faced official types (we called them "haircuts" when I was a kid in the West—talking about deputy sheriffs). Three rope-haired, dusty-legged young men and a woman were guarding the gate into the camp-ground. They were a decade younger than my own children; I wondered if everybody was taking names, or what? And I didn't get out of my rented Toyota; I didn't speak to any-body except that Montana patrolman. "Just driving around," I said. I wondered if he wrote down my license, if I would be checked out back at Budget Car Rental at the Jackson airport. The odor of new-cut alfalfa reminded me of child-hood mornings when it was easy to know what I thought.

Who did the patrolman imagine I was? Adult citizen on a public road? Was that good enough? Was it clear I was disgusted with my government and myself and about to cause an old-fart scene? I wondered if the people in the VW bus were being harassed, if they were anarchist bad-asses with their names all over FBI lists; I wondered why I wasn't anything but pissed off at myself. "I don't want my name on your lists," I told the patrolman. To hell with all of you, I thought, cursing my culture, you don't get to have my name. This is public land; these are public roads; and they belong to me and my people. I don't need to be on your lists; I don't need your stinking badges.

Remember the old stories about native people who were afraid to be photographed? They thought their souls were being stolen. I felt like that. There I was in the valley of the Madison River, and somebody was trying to steal my soul. Remember grade school, when they started telling you about Manifest Destiny? Did you sense a rat? Did it ever sound like the same story you heard around the house, from adults, in which power equals wisdom? Jefferson would have loved this land at the far edge of his Louisiana Purchase. More important, he likely he would have thought well of those radical children. Jefferson wrote, "I hold it a little re-bellion now and then is a good thing, and as necessary in the political world as storms in the physical."

And, he wrote, "The tree of liberty must be refreshed from time to time with the blood of patriots and tyrants."

There we were, me and the other *haircuts,* trying to love this gorgeous morning across the world in our way. I hated my own incapacities; I hit the road; I was out of there.

Let's try one more turn at making story. Under an early-winter moon it is possible to imagine witnessing the world in ancient clear-minded ways, without the dreaded self-conscious irony of the literate classes. There is not a single electric light in this dream. We study the stars and remember their old patterns as remnants of a language we forgot a long time ago, when the animals all knew how to lie down with one another (metaphorically, anyway).

In the West our society has never been fair (our ways have been notoriously imperialistic, sexist, and racist); and now our society is spinning apart (again). Men like my grandfather and even my father were furious; they had conspired all their lives to fashion a society that suited them. My mother was the boss's monied wife; she watched politicians on the TV news and laughed. "Those boys," she said.

The well is running dry. Where do we restart the continual process of remodeling ourselves and our culture? How do we understand the society forming around us? What is being made?

1) The West was an enormous empty (innocent?) stage waiting for a performance. Settlers believed that story. Sometimes they believed it was already a paradise, but more often they thought it was a place that needed remaking (irrigating).

2) The West has been performed (written) upon; we see the history of our performance everywhere; we see our societal and personal mythologies inscribed all over on the

landscape (fences, roads, canals, power lines, city plans, bomb ranges).

3) Many think that much of the West has been ruined. What does this mean—ruined in what sense—ecologically or politically or what? Ruined in terms of what models? Ruined by which kinds of miscalculations and injustices?

For openers, consider that the West was never empty in the first place. The story that we began with was nonsense. Is that the reason so much of what we experience around us resembles chaos (the emotional environs around Las Vegas)?

In *America* Baudrillard says America is a dream. Of course it is—life always is—we inhabit dreams. Then he says a thing that is more interesting: life in the American West is a dream of life after the crisis.

What was the crisis? "All that fascinates us is the *spectacle* of the brain and its workings." Out west we see a society in the midst of reinventing itself. Everyone is aware of this. We are all watching. An ironic society is trying to make itself up in a quite self-reflexive way. Our crisis is psychological, a crisis of awareness and guilt (through greed, we have ruined our paradise and we knew we were doing it), which has driven us to a deep sense of powerlessness. Anomie is the result (all that counts is selfishness; all actions are equal). In response to this crisis of will a society we don't understand is evolving with terrific speed (inscribing itself on us and our landforms).

So, here we are, out of control (again) after our semi-genocidal history of conquest and settlement. What to do? Maybe we want to live inside a new story, but how do we define it, how do we choose it, and how can we make it come to be?

On our first visit together in Glacier Park, Annick Smith and I and her twin boys, Alex and Andrew (they were about eleven at the time), hiked over 6 miles up to the Sperry Chalet, a 3,700-foot rise in elevation from the paved parking lot at the Lake McDonald Lodge. The boys ranged ahead like wolves when word came down the hill that we were in danger of missing supper. The second day we traipsed over to the Sperry Glacier, only about 4 miles and a 1,500-foot rise in elevation. The twins ran their eleven-year-old routes. Annick and I rested on the cool glacial ice. For a while we didn't notice the condom. It had been used and tossed away. Collapsed, it was slippery and luminous in the morning; someone had been testing our ice. Couples wandered the glacier and Annick wondered who it could have been—them, or them? I wondered exactly how much self-absorbed theatricality had been involved. It was my way of condescending to the moment. Sometimes I live to see the single thing light up. But when I am hounded and strange, looking to hide and perfect my revenge (my living well), then I cleave to obsessive purity, another place to be, in which nothing is forgiven.

Above trees in stony highlands it is possible to imagine that the absolute clarity of crystalline light over glacial cirques is a moral imperative to be nothing but correct—it is a way of killing possibility. We should go out under the blue-white skies, throw down a blanket, and make love on the glaciers (and carry out the parts that are not biodegradable). We are a far way into devastation of the interwoven system of life on our planet—the single environment in which our species will ever be able to live. As we seek ways to stop that devastation we think it is an enterprise of uttermost urgency. We at least think we are trying to save the world, which is a particularly powerful way of saving ourselves.

We are reinventing our notion of what is most valuable to us, as individuals and as a species, redefining what we take to be sacred; it is our most urgent business, our major communal enterprise. We are afraid of trying to exist on some starship, alone in the universe; we refuse to go on with business as usual. If we have some luck, if we want to believe (and why not?), and stay smart as we can, we may someday find ourselves living inside the solace of a coherent self. Miners and cowhands and unmarried mothers and married mothers and insurance salesmen and old female tattoo artists and nature freaks and timber-fallers and everyday downtown drunks and so on unto glory: we all have to learn empathy (so we try to tell ourselves) and cherish and forgive one another.

A man went to an abandoned house where he had lived with his family and found a bird, trapped inside the empty white-painted rooms, batting at the windows. Sunny spaces where the man had run to his mother as a child were thick with this terror. When he opened the windows, and the bird escaped, that was no cure.

Imagine meadowlarks and magpies coming down from their trees to look in our windows at night and study us in our sleep, and then flying away. Tomorrow we must sing to them, the birds say, because nothing else ever helps.

Bulletproof

It is often said that something may survive of a person after his death, if that person was an artist and put a little of himself into his work. It is perhaps in the same way that a sort of cutting taken from one person and grafted onto the heart of another continues to carry on its existence even when the person from whom it has been detached has perished.

—Marcel Proust, *Remembrance of Things Past*

THIS IS NO DOUBT a strange way to begin a story about traveling to visit Ray Carver, who had just missed dying. Or, as it turned out, not escaped. In fact he was dying. But of course we all are. That was what I told myself. In December of 1987, just after Christmas, Annick and I drove the freeways from Montana to visit my children and grandchildren and friends in Seattle. We ate fresh oysters; we played at frivolity and the idea that it is possible to live without guilt amid pleasures; we tried to ignore the idea that Ray was dying not so far away, at least I did; then Annick and I drove over to Port Angeles on the Olympic Peninsula, where Tess Gallagher and Ray were seeing to what was the end of his life. The rhododendron were flowering, and the azalea (or so it seems in memory), and Ray was fragile (a large, awkward man gone breakable), but not at all what you would think of as killed. Annick and I bought cut flowers in a shop on the main street in Port Angeles and took them up through the incessant rain to Ray's old-fashioned two-story house on the hill above the harbor. Ray made us some of his good coffee (he'd gone to coffee when he quit booze; coffee was his specialty). We sat in the bright kitchen with cut flowers on the drain board and drank the coffee and pretty soon we were talking. It was raining and quiet and Ray told us his story about healing from the unimaginable operation—the removal of about two-thirds of one cancerous lung. He'd coughed up blood one November morning in a kind of innocent, almost painless way, and the nightmare began. That was how he put it. "It was a nightmare," Ray said. Sunlight broke through, casting streaks of gunmetal brilliance across the seawater toward Vancouver Island. He smiled. "But now we're all right," he said. Something like that.

I watched Ray as if he were in possession of some secret message I could read if only I could pay close enough attention. The thought did not last but a second, a sort of forgettable twinge I put away as if such self-interest while face-on with the oncoming death of a friend were shameful. I was looking for a message that had to do with taking care by cherishing what there was to cherish, moment into moment. There was a secret Ray knew, and I didn't, a story he had learned. That evening Annick and I were alone in Ray's house. I sat in the chair where Ray sat when he read; I held his books and opened them to places where he had closed them. There was a tape deck, classical tapes. I played Vivaldi and tried to fathom this man who had been my friend in another life, before he was dying; I was trying to hear what he heard, as he heard it. He was reading mostly European poets. Milosz, others I can't remember. I'm moved to think of Philip Levine:

> Earth is eating trees, fence posts,
> Gutted cars, earth is calling in her little ones.
> ....
> They Lion grow.

Ray had stared himself down in the mirror of his imagination, and now he was dying without allowing himself to descend into any rattled bitterness so far as I could discern. I was trying to see how he got to where he was, trying to understand how it could be that he could absorb the terrifying joke of this perfect metaphysical injustice into his calmness and turn it reasonable, turn it into something no more unnatural than running water that drowns some mother's blessed child.

Ray and I had been friends since the spring of 1970. We liked to tell ourselves, as he said, that we had *seen some things*. We met one spring evening in the old Olympic Hotel in Seattle, perfectly by accident, and we fell for each other as inebriates will; we were playmates in love with the same possibilities. There was some college comp-class English teachers' gathering in the Olympic, and the lobby was given over to a display of books, a hundred or so yards of publishers' booths. But it was empty when I wandered through in the early evening, except for one scruffy fellow who was way down the line. As I was looking through a book of stories from literary magazines this fellow came up to my elbow and tried to look over my shoulder. "I've got a story in there," he said.

"Yeah," I said. "Bet you do."

"Raymond Carver," he said. I knew what he meant, but I didn't believe it. "It is," he said. "It's mine. Curt Johnson put it in there." This was not a lie anyone sensible would have bothered telling, at least in those days. It was clear this man was Raymond Carver, and I was one of the few people who would have found significance in that fact. This stranger had written a story called "Will You Please Be Quiet, Please?" It was famous in my mythologies. A couple of years before I had read that story in a hotel room in Portland, with my feet up on the bed, as I waited for my second wife to come back from somewhere; and that story had got me started again in my wondering if I had already ruined my life. "Will You Please Be Quiet, Please?" caused me to hang my head with heartbreak over my own situation in the world and yet to admire myself for even trying to confront those troubles as a writer.

However stupid it sounds, that's pretty close to what I thought right after I read "Will You Please be Quiet, Please?" one rainy afternoon in the old Benson Hotel in Portland while I yearned to be actual at something. For a little moment that story led me to think I was doing the right thing with my life. And here I was, better yet, in another hotel, with the guy who wrote the story. This was indeed the life; we were shy for some moments, then we touched, we shook hands, we talked about cups of coffee. Wait a minute, he said, why not a beer? I said, why not a drink? A drink would be fine, maybe a couple of drinks, what the hell, all things lay before us. It was that moment between drunks known as "Exchanging Credentials." Would you have a drink? Well, maybe, sure.

Even on the morning of this writing, a brilliant blue day that began with the temperatures well below zero, after an evening of Christmas celebration with family, I think of the old days and going down to the taverns in Missoula to join people I know. They are still there, some of them, and I still love their company. There was a time when we would be drunk by noon.

Days after Christmas, in the taverns, were always splendid in their timelessness. At heart loomed long hours of irresponsibility. It was possible to believe we were invisible and shatterproof, that we were walking on water for a while and beautiful in our souls. But those afternoons are gone. Ray took a hard fall on the booze. Drink was his secret companion in a more profound way than anything, even love, ever really works for most of us.

We pulled our tricks. It was our sport, and it would never end; we were free and invulnerable. During June of 1973, running on getaway bravado and whiskey, I took a long run from Missoula and found myself at Carver's house in Cupertino. On my first day in town we made our way over to a literary party in Berkeley, in some public room on the campus. I found myself talking to a famous critic with a glass of white wine in my hand and thinking in my drunken self-pretense that I knew some never-before-revealed thing about *texts*. Ray lifted a sack of ice over his head, crashed it down on the corner of a trestle table, and three half-gallons of gin danced off to shatter on the stone floor. We hired a graduate student to drive us back to Cupertino. And we lived there a week in dreams drinking two bottles of vodka every day—one for each of us. In the morning I would come out of my bedroom to find Ray in the living room with vodka, orange juice, ice—my drink mixed. Toward the end of the week we wandered up to the liquor store at the high end of Cupertino Road, where we had been taking turns on buying the booze, and ordered a half-gallon. "Christ," the clerk said. "You guys together?"

Crossing the twilight of a moving-picture six-plex parking lot on the west side of San Jose, I looked back to see Maryann looking back another fifty yards to Ray beside their little yellow Japanese automobile. He had waited until we moved off toward the theater, then come up with a pint from under the seat, and now he was downing the last of it, chin to the China pink of the evening sky and oblivious to us in what he thought of as his selfishness.

That fall Ray taught full-time in Iowa City, in the Writers' Workshop with the likes of John Cheever. He felt as if maybe he were some semblance of the real thing since there he was there with Cheever, who was damned sure the real thing and as much a drunk as anybody.

Every Friday afternoon Ray was supposed to meet a beginning poetry writing class at College V, UC Santa Cruz. It was possible; he could fly from Iowa City on Thursday, meet his class, and fly back to meet his Iowa workshop on Tuesday. He'd worked a deal with one of the airlines—free tickets for an essay (which of course never got written) in the airline magazine.

No problem. Two jobs, two paychecks, home every weekend. And he showed up on the airplane each Thursday evening for a number of weeks. Always drunk. I had left my second wife behind in Missoula and was thrashing around in the single life again, temporarily, according to my plans anyhow, at Stanford with a Stegner Fellowship. So I was available, and I drove him down the fifty or so miles to Santa Cruz, and he ceremoniously pinned a notice to the door of his classroom: *Can't teach. Sick.* And it was true. The next week Ray lay down in the backseat of my car so no one could possibly see him, and it was my job to pin up the notice. The next week Chuck Kinder and I went down without Ray. The class was mostly barefoot hippie children. We faced a circle of their grass-stained feet propped up around a conference table. Kinder refused to look. I carried on like some prideful pissant. That was the last of those classes; Ray stopped coming altogether.

That Christmas there was a swaying in warm winds; Ray flew to Missoula, then he drove south with my second wife and Ed McClanahan, who was taking my place in

Missoula. It seemed like we all might couple up again and make peace and be lovey. And we kind of did, for a week or so. Ray and Maryann looked to be bemused by happiness as they drifted off from a small party at McClanahan's house in Palo Alto. It wasn't until the next day that I got a full report. It was one of our sports in those days, the full report.

Ray had lost Maryann. I mean lost her. He drove twenty some freeway miles from McClanahan's to their place in Cupertino, innocently, without Maryann. He left her standing at the curb; the car door was locked on her side. Rather than come back into McClanahan's, Maryann hitched a ride with an old couple. There were lots of rides hitched in those days. The old couple drove Maryann to her door. Ray was at the refrigerator. "Oh," he said, when Maryann came in the door. "I wondered where you were." The full report. Ray said he was slicing an onion, a Walla Walla Sweet, for a sandwich. Later on he didn't eat. That was a way you told the beginning of the end; people stopped eating.

Maybe Ray was the more easily wounded, maybe he was physically fragile, or maybe he was simply capable of taking all of what was happening more seriously than most of us and saw through our joke in a clearer way. Maybe he was more open to wounding, witnessing what became our war zone with a heart not so securely boarded up and barricaded as, at the least, was mine.

Maybe Ray recognized that in the long run we weren't reaping freedom after all; maybe we had been tricked. I hope there's not anything about this recital of antics that sounds prideful, like the kind of stories you dine out on. Once they were, once I used them that way. I recall telling them in bars while we all had a swell time; they had a certain currency.

Ray suffered a sight of chaos deep in his soul, turned away and sobered up in the middle 1970s, and moved up the coast to McKinleyville, just north of the little university town of Arcadia, where he had gone to school in the old days. Friends like Dick Day helped him through the drying out. I visited a couple of times, on my way to San Francisco. I asked Ray if he was writing. By this time he'd been sober for most of a year. "No," he said. "I could. But I'm not."

I asked him why. "Because I can't convince myself it's worth doing." That surprised me. I thought about it for days. It implied a kind of consequence I had never anticipated. We had seen a lot by then, but it never seemed possible that even the fractured marriages and falling-down, bite-your-tongue convulsions could lead to such seriousness. Ray must have witnessed phantoms I had not imagined. I believed in work, and if that was not worth doing, well then, there was no way to make good on anything; there was no justifying anything. I let myself believe that good writing was like a license to steal; anything was forgivable so long as you were writing well. It's a line of bullshit a lot of people like me have used to excuse endless rudeness and selfishness, cruelty and cheap-shit misconduct; a line so stupid and demeaning I wonder if I believed it at the time.

This is what I think: no one thing justifies any other thing. Each thing you do stands alone; they don't add up, not in any direction; nothing accumulates. There is no magic; the work you do is work you got done, good or bad, and it doesn't earn you any moral advantage. No points. If you have the good luck to do good work, that's a fine thing. But it has nothing to do with making you anything but lucky.

A lot of long-term Sunday-afternoon sadness in taverns where I go, among people I know, has to do with wasted possibilities. Fine and capable people who didn't do any work and collapsed into serving their own selves and plea-sures, as I was inclined, for so long. Drunk in the morning. Those were fine times, I have to say, with fine friends. I loved them dearly.

But it has been a good idea, for me, to attempt putting away indulgence and make-believe and to try to identify decencies to serve, not god or country but community, which is a larger, extended version of our own selves. We are responsible; nothing is bulletproof.

These weren't thoughts I let myself dwell on in those days. Most of what I did was support a set of all-day excuses for seldom working. Maybe Ray saw visions; maybe that was his trouble. Maybe he had the heebie-jeebies and scared himself. But I was not scared.

And there we were, not many years later; he was famous, and dying, and I was studying him for hints. In the months before his affliction revealed itself Ray had taken to inspecting condominiums on the hills of Seattle overlooking Elliot Bay and shipping lanes to the Orient. The condos were right near the Public Market with its perfect produce and living geoducks you could kill and fry for dinner and flowers picked just that morning. He liked to talk about living close to amenities. Just out the windows you could witness sunset over the Olympic Mountains. This was the saw-filer's son from Yakima, and he was getting his chance at the world. He wanted properties.

In the fall of 1982, I was visiting in southern Vermont. Ray showed up driving an immaculate new Mercedes. He had been going home to Syracuse from John Gardner's funeral and had decided you might as well enjoy the things you could afford. "So what the hell," he said. "I bought this car. Who knows?" That was what we were all studying, on that visit to Port Angeles when he was dying: "Who knows?"

What I was concerned about, that last time, was watching myself as I watched Ray, studying him, envying his equilibrium. He had survived some series of transformations, and I wanted to share the wisdom, if it was wisdom. Ray was dying, and I wanted to know how he could conduct himself as he did; I wanted to see what he saw when he looked out from his seashore to the flow of his ocean. I wanted to hear his music as he heard it.

The summer before, I'd gone to Port Angeles for the salmon fishing. It all seemed so easy, that dream, and natural enough. We caught salmon, the day was brilliant. Ray was the generous center of it all, our prince of good fortune and proof that some rewards were justly rationed out by the way of things. And now his life was over, soon now, forever. Someone had canceled his ticket to the rest of the party.

On a bright chill morning, Ray and Tess and Annick and I took a short hike on a path to the edges of the beach, where we were stopped by driftwood logs. Ray was still healing from his operation and moving like an old man. He refused to climb over the logs, and we turned inland along the fairways of a golf course bordering a tiny creek and looped back over a bridge across the river. It was an expedition into the native world. Back at Tess's house, Ray opened a tin of canned salmon; we ate a little, and that is what there is to tell. There is no insight here, no moment, no recognition; there is just my friend in his gentle patience with his terrible fate, and with us. Ray could have been impatient, thinking we were using up what little remained of his life. Maybe he did. Or maybe he was glad of the company.

On August 3, 1988, in warm morning sunlight on a patio outside a mental-health clinic in Aspen, Colorado, I was meeting a fiction-writing class. "I see in the paper," one of them said, "where your friend is dead." He was talking about the *New York Times*. Ray was dead at fifty, leaving the example of his conduct while dying.

In December of 1988, coming home from the beaches

near La Push, Annick and I passed a chaos of clear-cut logging debris near the town of Forks: heedless wreckage, mile-long swatches of torn earth and jagged rotting stump-age of the cedar trees, limbs crushed into black mud, the earth perfectly violated. We stopped in Port Angeles and visited the highland over the seacoast where Ray is bur-ied. Tess had worn a little path around the grave. She went down and talked to him, she said. I tell him the news, she said. Like all of us, Ray was given to a love of gossip and scandal. His eyes would gleam; he would lean into the talk. But as I stood there by his grave I had nothing much in the way of things to say to the dead, except to make a game of my question. How is it, sport? I was too scared for much fun with the news. Later, following Ray, I went to Anton Chekhov and found this passage from "Gooseberries."

I said to myself: how many happy, contented people there really are! What an overwhelming force they are! Look at life: the insolence and idleness of the strong, the ignorance and brutishness of the weak, horrible poverty everywhere, overcrowding, de-generation, drunkenness, hypocrisy, lying—Yet in all the houses and on all the streets there is peace and quiet; of the fifty thousand people who live in our town there is not one who would cry out, who would vent his indignation aloud. We see the people who go to market, eat by day, sleep by night, who babble nonsense, marry, grow old, good-naturedly drag their dead to the cemetery, but we do not see those who suffer and what is terrible in life goes on everywhere behind the scenes. Everything is peaceful and quiet and only mute statistics protest: so many gallons of vodka drunk, so many children dead from malnutrition—And such a state of things is evidently necessary; obviously the happy man is at ease only because the unhappy ones bear their burdens in silence, and if there were not this silence, happiness would be impossible. It is a general hypnosis. Behind the door of every contented, happy man there ought to be someone standing with a little hammer and continually reminding him with a knock that there are unhappy people, that however happy he may be, life will sooner or later show him its claws, and trouble will come to him—illness, poverty, losses, and then no one will see or hear him, just as now he neither sees nor hears others. But there is no man with a hammer. The happy man lives at his ease, faintly fluttered by small daily cares, like an aspen in the wind, and all is well.

Chekhov understood that stories, when they are valuable, are open in their willingness to make universal metaphors from our personal difficulties. Our most useful stories focus simultaneously on our generous and betraying ways. These troubles could be yours, the story says, this unfairness *is* yours, and so are these glories.

Ray must have spent time listening to Chekhov's person with the little hammer. It is easy to see that his most profound sympathies lay with the disenfranchised, the saw-filers like his father, as did Chekhov's. Ray's last story, "Errand," about the death of Chekhov, drinking champagne as you die, and celebrating what we have, which is this, what we have. It is one of his put-yourself-in-my-shoes, try-my-blindness stories, in which people make a try at understanding and even being *someone else.* Ray gave the world what strength and decency he could muster and died out of a foreshortened life (as we do; each of us). By his time of dying Ray had come to what seemed an objectified sense of his beliefs; he implied, sure enough, sadness all over town—but, like my man Chekhov, I'm going to forgive myself and try on happiness anyway. However misguided our lives may have been, we pray that they may be ultimately forgivable. My culture poured burning napalm on babies, on purpose. The human story can at one level be understood as a history of conquest, law-bringing, and violence. Much of what we do is madness. But our story can also be understood as a weave of suffering and compassion, joyousness and reverence. Somebody should write up a history of compassion and forgiveness and caretaking that emphasizes the value of intimacy.

Ray's best work suggests the need for keeping decent while deep amid our own consternations. His stories are masterworks of usefulness; they lead us to imagine what it is like to be another person. It's the great thing: in intimacy we learn to cherish one another through acts of the imagination. Nothing could be more political.

Death and a Wedding

For Pat Kittredge and James Welch

TALKING TOGETHER, my brother Pat and I made up a story, and—to some degree—as a consequence he's dead. Pat was sixty-seven years old, a defunct lawyer living paycheck to paycheck. His life was centered on golf and working nights on the maintenance crew at the University of Montana. Over a couple of months, he developed pains in his upper back, to the point where he couldn't sleep. So he took pain pills, bought a new mattress, and went to a chiropractor. When the pain got worse, he went to a doctor who advised him to take stronger over-the-counter pain pills. He was worried about losing his job—his independence. And I was worried about him, but not to the point of interfering.

At last we decided he should go to the Emergency Room at St. Patrick's Hospital in Missoula, where the response was immediate, and—one supposes—expert. By midafternoon he had two stents in an artery and was in a hospital room where he stayed four days while doctors kept an eye on what they called a "stunned" response on the part of his heart. It wasn't beating to the right beat, yet. But it soon would, the doctors assured him of that. The doctors said he had "dodged a bullet" and would soon be feeling better than he had in years. Out of the hospital on a Sunday, on Monday Pat was fitted with a harness to monitor his heart for another twenty-four hours. We spent that afternoon together—a sweet time—laughing and talking. Everything was going to be fine.

But the next day he didn't answer the telephone. By evening I was worried (terrified) and went to his apartment. There was no answer to the doorbell. A good man from the rental agency let me in, and there was Pat, dead in his sleep according to the monitor he was wearing, at 1:30 the night before on that new mattress—Pat, my brother and closest friend. Through these events Pat and I acted in good faith, doing what we saw to be the right thing according to the stories we used to order our world and to reassure ourselves. Annick had suggested weeks before that maybe his pains had to do with his heart, but we didn't listen. He and I had been acting out a hopeful story about our lives going on as usual that turned out to be deadly, and Pat was dead. We miss him like crazy.

ॐ

Living in the French Quarter of New Orleans, Annick and I were walking in the rain when we heard echoes of someone singing, an unaccompanied voice in the narrow street, maybe four blocks away when I first heard her. She was a young black woman with her eyes closed and face open to the rain as her voice rose and fell to "Glory, Glory, Hallelujah."

She shone in the gray light. I almost couldn't look and wondered if she cared what anybody thought as I dropped two folded paper dollars into the coffee can at her feet. She didn't look at me at all.

In a place where everything was carpentered our shuttered door was one in a wall of shuttered doors, each painted thick green, stretching toward Bourbon Street. Gray light illuminating wet bricks rebounded from the walls.

I can still hear that woman, whose life looked to be

endlessly more difficult than mine. Her courage and her passion were evident in her singing. I envied her strength and felt as if I might weep, for myself, and I was fearful, as if something in me might break. I was awash with sadness nearby to some of the best eating and drinking and music anywhere, in a place where I never heard so many people—black, white, Creole, Cajun—laughing so much of the time.

Maybe it was because I had never lived so close to so much violence, which was the other side of things. During Mardi Gras, on Rampart Street, a little more than three blocks from our door, some lost tourist was shot every night, killed and robbed. Every week or so there was a schoolyard killing, a kid assassinating another kid with a handgun, settling scores.

The perpetrators in these crimes were most often young men from the so-called "projects," public housing for the poor. Those men were alienated and angry because they saw that their situation was hopeless—they were essentially uneducated, their schools were war zones, and their chances of finding jobs, much less meaningful, respected work, were nil.

A friend who grew up in New Orleans said, "They've got no place to go. There's no ladder up, no ladder out. They're left with nothing but selfishness. It's the second lesson you learn on the streets." The first lesson, according to my friend, is that nothing, nobody, is bulletproof.

A lot of people are staring back at us, the enfranchised, with hatred, which we all know to be at least partway justifiable. Fewer and fewer of them are willing to stand singing in the rain, waiting for a few dollars to accumulate in the tin can at their feet.

⌒

For unknown but undoubtedly awful reasons, on the streets of Nogales, Annick and I were beset by beggars. Mexico, we think. Most of us shrug off Mexican tragedies as inevitable. But they're the result of policies. Dealings along the border have more than ever been inhumanely commodified since the North American Free Trade Agreement—an executive agreement—"opened" the border to many economic transactions.

It's proposed that the border be entirely opened. But that's not likely in any foreseeable future; citizens across the Southwest are infuriated and terrified by the idea of their towns and economies being overwhelmed by thousands upon thousands, maybe millions, of immigrants.

In any event, a lot of goods cross without paying tariffs. So both economies benefit; that's the theory. But it hasn't been an entirely win-win deal. Good jobs in the United States were moved to Mexico to be taken by workers earning less than minimum wage.

CEOs in the United States, interested in locating production facilities where wages are cheap and environmental constraints are not serious, set up factories in borderland Mexico, directly connected to U.S. highways. General Motors closed plants in the United States and Canada and became the largest employer in Mexico. Factories in Mexico, called *maquiladoras*, paint Fords, make steering wheels, brake shoes, entire Volkswagens, toasters, Sony TVs, ATMs, modems, you name it, and shorten their workers' lives by regarding environmental heedlessness as a way of doing business.

Thousands of Mexican citizens have moved north in order to work in the *maquiladoras*, and trucks bearing "goods" produced with cheap Mexican labor enter the United States by the thousands every day. It's a system in which the corporations, and their customers, exploit the poor. In my own case, ducking away from the beggars in Nogales is typical of my relationship to the Mexican poor; ultimately our relationship is much like a dealing between a master and slaves.

Meanwhile, the Mexican economy is driven by a "shadow market" in cocaine, heroin, medicines, pesticides banned in the USA, cowboy boots made of endangered sea-turtle flippers, and laundered money. The cocaine trade, it's said, is worth twice the profits of the Mexican petroleum industry. The police in Sinaloa, below the western border, are said to cooperate with the drug dealers; they are not simply corrupt, they are in fact another batch of criminals. Mexico goes increasingly outlaw as a result of pandering to U.S. appetites.

Hundreds of thousands migrate, or attempt to migrate, into the United States. The most lucrative racket, after dealing drugs and laundering money, is forging U.S. visas. It's claimed that 60 percent of the retail economy in Douglas and Nogales turns on drugs, and 25 percent of the economy in Tucson. The war on drugs, if it were to succeed, might destroy the economy in Mexico (not to speak of Tucson).

Eight hundred thousand Mexicans cross the border legally, daily, some flashing plastic cards that constitute a visa. Some have seasonal jobs; others go shopping at Wal-Mart (the Wal-Mart in Laredo, Texas, has the highest per-square-foot sales of any in the world; Wal-Mart's sales equal the total GNP of the world's ninety-three smallest national economies). Immigrants take jobs nobody else wants, and then they go home to sleep. That's fine with everybody at U.S. Immigration.

But there are many who don't qualify for visas. They are poor and uneducated, often from the villages. They have no economic ties to anyone really except a family that they can best serve by sending money from the U.S. They're seen as bad risks to overstay any kind of visa and are semi-automatically rejected. Most don't bother to apply.

Four or five thousand are caught trying to cross the border illegally every twenty-four hours. Around Douglas, in March 1999, Border Patrol agents arrested 61,000—almost 100 per hour. Others die trying, and they haunt us—sad eager people who hire a "coyote" to smuggle them across the border. We don't want to think about those who perish while locked in the trunk of an automobile or those who wander the deserts unto death without water in 120-degree heat.

But thousands who try to cross the border succeed. They travel north to work as pickers, gardeners, and motel maids, domestic servants, ranch hands, and garbage men. They, again, are not really a problem. Lots of Americans love to hire them because they're willing to work at jobs nobody else wants, for less than a minimum wage, and to maintain a very low profile.

Our answer to the "problem" of illegal immigrants, like our answer to that other problem driven by desire— drugs—is a "war." The battle against illegal immigrants, like the war on drugs, is against a tide that's not likely to subside in the foreseeable future. It's obviously an ongoing failure— inhumane and foolish.

Street theory has it that illegal immigrants, like the flow of drugs, constitute an unsolvable problem. That's also nonsense. Long-term humane solutions don't lie with "wars" or trickle-down NAFTA economics. Responsible ways of dealing with borderland troubles, to succeed, must center on *giving*, by citizens and governments, and by the corporations that buy and sell on both sides of the border. The poor must be cut in on the economic action.

National governments and the corporations could institute a system of economic stimulus and social aid aimed directly toward the disenfranchised in the urban ghettos and backland villages. But there'd be no quick fixes; there'd be millions of attempts at graft, many of which would succeed; it would take generations and big-time funding.

But morale among the Mexican public, and democratic behavior in the Mexican government, might eventually evolve. Mexican citizens might generate the will to clean up their banking and justice systems and put the lid on graft. It's a choice. Otherwise, we're looking at increasing social and moral chaos. The world can't be bullied into order.

Conditions along the border are already out of control. Study the photos collected in *Juárez: The Laboratory of Our Future*, with text by Charles Bowden, introduction by Noam Chomsky, and an afterword Eduardo Galeano (whose *Memory of Fire* trilogy is the necessary text for anyone interested in the underside of history in the Americas).

"The precarious equilibrium of the world," Galeano writes, "which teeters on the brink of the abyss, depends on the perpetuation of injustice. The misery of the many makes possible the extravagance of the few."

There are photographs of desiccated bodies: many of them—the murdered—were people involved in drug deals gone wrong, or women who were raped and killed. Their graves, dug in the sand, have been uncovered by the wind. There are children harvesting the city dumps, contesting with dogs and goats for what food they can find. "In Juárez," Charles Bowden writes, "you cannot sustain hope." I'm driven, eyeing those photos, to nausea. Sneaking glances, I see why so many are so frantic to escape. Why so many, worldwide, are so furious as we exclude them from the first-world party. Then I look away, as we mostly do. The book protests horrifying realities, a future we're likely to have—privileged and alone, increasingly isolated, barricaded in enclaves around the world as the poor wander furiously in denuded homelands, plotting revenge.

"Once we needed immigrants, we welcomed them," a man at a party said. "Now we don't need them, so we wall them out and call them barbarians. One of these days, like they did to Rome, they're going to come after us."

We need to consider the rage generated by disenfranchisement and a pervasive sense of hopelessness. It starts with promises. People come to us thinking they have been promised freedom and opportunity, the chance to invent a new, fruitful life. But that story often doesn't come true. The result is alienation: people who feel excluded from what their society defines as the prime rewards of life. They sense that they are utterly out of the loop. In the rural outback, and in the deep heartlands of the cities, they turn to heedless anger.

Many of us live with a sense that there is something deeply wrong in our society, that our culture has lost track of the fundamental reasons why one thing is more significant than another. We are fearful and driven to forget the most basic generosities. We anesthetize ourselves with selfishness. It's not, we say, our fault.

Many of us live insulated, as I do much of the time. In New Orleans I like to walk down a couple of blocks to the Bombay Club and disassociate my sensibilities with one and then another huge perfect martini. In Las Vegas I like to stay at the brilliantly named Mirage, amid the orchids and white tigers.

I want to think I deserve what I get. I don't want to consider how vastly I am overrewarded, or the injustices around me. I don't want encounters with the disenfranchised. I want to say it is not my fault. But it is—it's mine, and ours. We'd better figure out ways to spread equity around if we want to go on living in a world that is at least semi-functional. It's a responsibility, to ourselves. We inhabit a complex culture that is intimately connected to societies over the world. A culture of the wealthy, and increased polarization between rich and poor. Our culture is multiethnic, multiracial, predominately urban, ironic, self-reflexive, drug-crazed, dangerous, and resounding with discordant energies. We've become a selfish inhumane society without a coherent myth to believe in, and we are coming unglued. Our democracy is failing. Many of its citizens do not believe in it anymore; they don't vote—withdrawing from the processes of governing themselves. On C-SPAN, all day long, you will see the other end of that same society: privileged long-faced citizens trying to figure out what to do about our trouble without forgoing their privileges. You will see a society without much idea of how to proceed.

I want to inhabit a story in which the animals all lie down with one another; everybody is satisfied; and children play on sandy beaches by a stream, in the warm shade of the willows, the flash of salmon in the pools. Children of your own as you see them. Such glories. What to do? How do we understand our kingdom? Stories about business as usual don't serve us very well; they never did. Let's hope they don't get us killed.

◌

We are all responsible for evoking and naming the world as accurately as we can—as it glows in light and hides in the darkness, as it reeks and breeds, smells and feels and is understood by stockbrokers and farmers, housewives and miners, loggers, laughing boys and dancing girls and single mothers and scientists; as it is used by men and women of every persuasion. As we try to define our true situation it is our responsibility to make our arguments as clearly as possible while at the same time recognizing that it's almost impossible to get beyond subjectivity.

It's easy to see that the world is luminous and significant. We want those significances to be part of the story of our life. We yearn to live in a coherent place we can name, where we can feel safe.

Many of our most deeply held myths, when acted out, result in indifference to the fates of others, and result in fearfulness and defensiveness, and warfare, conquest, and revenge—all of which are proving to be increasingly dysfunctional attitudes and ways of proceeding in a world that refuses to be beaten or bullied into order.

We can be both profoundly creative and destructive, often simultaneously. Our best and worst impulses come out of our commonplace need to heal and complete ourselves, and then do it again.

My brother Pat died in part because of bad luck, the fragility of things, and in part because he and I acted out a story that didn't serve him well. He and I were thus led to think in ways that were inattentive and inflexible.

There will never be a simple program or set of programs to help us serve and preserve glories, but it might be useful if we heard more about the rewards of taking care—stories about humor, attentiveness, and flexibility—and not an endlessness of the self-righteous combat stories we now get from our anxious culture. Stories about the arts of building fortresses, revenge, and triumph are every time about divisiveness, and semi-suicidal in an increasingly interdependent world. We can decide to dedicate ourselves to taking care. Many do. It's said to be like learning an art.

The Next Rodeo

JUST AFTER WORLD WAR II, fourteen and wind-burned after a summer on the greasewood and lava-rock deserts of southeastern Oregon, I was given the honor of helping buckaroos from the MC Ranch drive a dozen saddle horses over the Warner Mountains to Lakeview and the Labor Day Rodeo. My grandfather picked me for that horse drive. He was a stocky, blue-eyed man who'd come up from a starve-out salt-flat ranch to own an empire of horses and thousands of cows. It was common in his world to imagine that property would heal wounds, including emotional isolation. "Any time we got ahead, he bought cows." That lament came from my grandmother after she had outlived him by a decade. Men like him, in rodeo parades behind flag-bearers and the queen and her white-hat court, were kings of the mountain in that country, at that time.

Cantering from a canyon east of town, we drove our clattering iron-shod herd onto asphalt streets leading to the stockyards. Men from the far ends of the county, afoot on the sidewalks, rolled cigarettes and eyed us. But the kids, that was what I liked. There were kids my age running among square-backed automobiles parked diagonally along the curbs, and maybe they were wondering about me, another kid on horseback alongside heroes: young fellows like Casper Gunderson and Rossie Dollarhide who'd be coming out of the bucking chutes in the saddle-bronc finals on Monday afternoon.

After unsaddling and graining our horses, we piled into a battered army-surplus jeep and went uptown to a tavern where a bartender set me up with a bottle of beer. There I was, elbow to elbow with men I dreamed of growing up to resemble. Manhood loomed.

Later, in the thronging lobby of the Lakeview Hotel, a yellow-haired ranch hand pawed at my mother's shoulder. She batted at him and screeched as she scrambled away, up the wide central stairway. The man followed. My father must have heard her. He came down the hall from their second-floor room in a half-buttoned dress shirt and his underwear to deliver a running right hook. The yellow-haired fellow staggered backwards into the railing and flopped over to land on the stairs below in an inert sprawl. It looked for a moment as if he might be actually dead. But his was only a drunk-man problem. My father got into his trousers and boots and went down to the hotel barroom to resolve the trouble. He shook the blond man's hand and bought him a drink. Then the yellow-haired fellow went off to the taverns, to that night maybe sleep in the Colorado Hotel, where the working stiffs were putting up two or three to a room. Or perhaps out to "Hollywood," on the far side of the rodeo grounds, where men rolled out their bedrolls in sagebrush between a half-dozen tar-paper shacks where prostitutes resided. In any event, "Back to his kind."

Hurdy-gurdy music blared from the carnival down the street as I lay down on a cot at the dark end of the hallway outside my parents' room. How quickly things could go sour. Some bad thing—what was it?—had got out of its box. But my father had nailed the lid back down.

Rodeos traditionally provided release and gabby communality for people isolated by physical and psychic distances.
There was bull- and wild-horse riding for the young fellows
and team roping for the older generation and backslapping
all around for the ranchers and field hands and log-truck
drivers and bunkhouse cooks and haberdashers and drug-
gists and full-time town drunks. Each sunup gimpy old
men drifted down from their hotel rooms to assemble on
the sidewalks and roll their first cigarette of the day. They
had traveled a lot of miles for the visiting and didn't want
to miss a lick of it.

Such assembling is a fading tradition. Families still gather
on the short-grass plains of eastern Montana for Sunday
brandings, and loggers dance to fiddle music in the Rockies.
But rodeo and the mythological West have been increasingly taken over by show business. In early January each year,
tens of thousands of rodeo fans gather in Las Vegas for the
National Finals. It's sort of a ranchland Super Bowl. Three
weeks later tourists and locals gather in Elko, Nevada, for
the "old-time" rowdy atmospherics that go with a weekend
of cowboy-poetry recitations—again, thousands of them.

Even so, westerners in the outback often feel that they
have been dealt out of their culture, economically and
psychically, that they are increasingly inconsequential. "We
work, and city people are having their payday."

⁓

North American peoples with cultures as distinct from one
another as the Sioux and Navajo and Iroquois lived complex lives hunting, gardening, gathering, warring, and governing for millennia. Then white explorers came along with
European diseases, followed by military horsemen with fire-
arms. Tribal people were for the most part either exterminated
or relocated. European settlers took their lands. The process

was speedy and merciless, and not at all exceptional in terms of world history.

In July 1847, Mormons had made their difficult way across distances in Wyoming to stand looking over the Great Salt Lake in Utah. Their leader, Brigham Young, said, "This is the right place." There they continue to make their stand. Almost exactly one hundred years later, in the classical Western, *Red River,* directed by Howard Hawks, a man named Thomas Dunson (played by John Wayne) found country in Texas free for the taking after the Civil War and said, as if claiming the rights to his life, "This is the place."

It's an American ritual, enacted over and over again. Moments when a homeland is found and claimed are central to stories of who Americans are. These are stories about earning freedom with work and loyalty, prudence and common sense, and courage if need be. Explorers and fur trappers, one-mule miners and travelers in wagon trains came west to realize dreams of freedom and prosperity. Wealth was for most of them the primary way of nailing down an identity—that notion held together what passes for a culture in the West through waves of successive frontiers. It's our locating myth, acted out over and over in the rude world and more often in dreams.

Ultimately, it often evolves into a story about class. The Lakeview rodeo was divided along such lines—propertied men and women found ways to lord their status and wealth over those without. Maybe there's a version of that story which might heal us. More likely it's a fiction that should be reimagined.

The American West is home to dozens of cultures and subcultures, native and from abroad. These groups are often as distinct from one another as the Irish from County Cork and the Basque from northern Spain. And just about as often at odds with their neighbors.

Germans out of Russia brought hard red wheat seed from the Volga River plow grounds and have prospered on the Great Plains since the 1860s. Laotians escaping the conflict in Vietnam came to the Bitterroot Valley of Montana in the 1970s. From the Hutterite colonies on the short-grass plains and oil geologists in Wyoming to Internet nerds in Boise to Latinos digging tunnels under the Arizona border in Douglas, western cultures are complexly evolving. Ideas of the right life presently exist in manifestations many find bizarre—tattooed skateboard addicts clatter off the ramps outside public buildings in Salt Lake City and citizens who've lost touch with all ethical responsibilities manufacture and sell crystal meth while their neighbors argue that evolution, biological or cultural, is an evil idea or anyway, nonsense.

At the same time, in counties across Montana and in the Dakotas and Nebraska, Kansas and Oklahoma, Colorado and west Texas, New Mexico and Arizona, disenfranchised but born-again Christian citizens are drifting into a political alignment with utterly unchurched rednecks. Together, they form a cadre of contemporary populists that shares feelings of exclusion from our national culture, a sense of neglect and resentment. They often vote these frustrations by electing people they see as of their own kind. These folk mainly come from conservative backgrounds, but they aren't likely to always support conservative social agendas since they are mostly poor, and the poor tend to favor spreading wealth around. If they can escape the boundaries of western bigotry and combine forces with the Latinos and Native Americans, they will bring a lot of votes—power—to western political futures. What will they want?

Simultaneously, semi-wealthy and well-educated new-comers are flocking into the West, particularly in economi-cally booming areas but also in the hideout boondocks. Many of these people, while nominally retired, are still energetic and looking for projects. They increasingly tend to band together and try to dominate local politics. Some of them are profoundly conservative, others powerful and liberal. It's equally hard to predict their ultimate influence. Who are we becoming in our West? Where are we going?

The nation tends to think of the West as predominately rural, but 80 percent of the 60 million citizens who call themselves "westerners" live in Tucson, Albuquerque, Phoenix, Denver and Colorado Springs, Boise, Reno, Las Vegas, and in metropolitan areas on the coast: Vancouver, Seattle, Portland, San Jose/San Francisco, and Los Angeles. Our three fastest-growing states, nationally, are Arizona, Nevada, and Idaho. Buckeye, Arizona, a dusty suburb on creosote flats west of Phoenix, is blossoming into a city of more than one million. Colorado Springs will be larger than Denver in a decade. Meanwhile, the historic "Old West" is increasingly enshrined in theatrical rodeos and museum di-oramas. An overwhelmingly urban population, with more in common with Manhattan than the horseback territory where I grew up, nevertheless still tends to name itself in terms of an antique mythos—the Western. The West flows with cultures, but none of its foundation stories are widely persuasive—not to speak of functional.

In fifty years, the major western cities are likely to be semi-unlivable because of petroleum and water shortages. If oil runs out, and there's every sign it will, there's no evi-dence that ethanol or hydrogen fuel or coal liquids and the like will seriously alleviate the crisis. Urban centers linked to their suburbs by automobile expressways are not systems likely to be remotely viable. Let's hope light-rail is at least partially workable. And metro centers in the southwestern deserts will become increasingly dysfunctional as water shortages worsen, particularly if droughts caused by global warning continue to materialize. Politicians don't like talk of water-supply shortfalls, but they are familiar with the problem. Desert cities are running dry and scrambling. Las Vegas has claimed enough water from the Colorado River to allow for the building of another 120,000 new homes a year from a river that's going dry before it reaches the Sea of Cortez. The city fathers in Vegas are scheming to divert water from northern Nevada, three hundred miles away. Tucson is trying to slow down the depletion of underground aquifers while developing water-conservation technologies. We hope Tucson politicians rise above denying the problem and prove willing to institute widely unpopular plans—like putting the brakes on economic development, shutting down golf courses, and drying up lawns across hundreds of subdivisions.

Urban populations live in neighborhoods. As in rural areas, they understand and value their neighbors. Urban citizens who inhabit areas quite unlike one another—inner-city ghettos and affluent suburbs, the poor and the well-to-do, the millions of them—are inevitably going to be calling the shots in the West. But they're likely to cancel one another out a lot of the time. The result will be endless varieties of political gridlock.

The most insistent western dreams center on finding a homeland and/or cornucopia. It lives in many hearts, even as the territory is plowed, mined, logged, and drilled and subdivided unto death. Meadows in remote creek valleys sell for "rich man's prices" to people coming to the West from the tattered glories of southern California and New

Jersey. Wealthy people flowed into Santa Fe and Taos a century ago, into Sun Valley during the 1930s and Aspen in the 1940s and into Jackson Hole and Sedona and other pristine sites, where they are given to building varnished log homes the size of railway depots. They own a lot of gates, and as a consequence, are widely despised by locals, which isn't altogether fair.

Many of the wealthy support good causes. They work to stamp out crystal-meth production in local trailer courts, donate food for poor indigenous children, and give money to fund the preservation of grizzly and wolf habitats and pintail-duck nesting sites in the prairie pothole areas of the Dakotas and Saskatchewan (without, of course, forgoing their privileges). With grievous exceptions, many see clearly that it's sensible, and even necessary, to care for their adopted homeland. Otherwise, where next, which island?

Upper-middle-class retirees sell a house in Orange County for a million bucks. They replace it in the Bitterroot Valley of Montana for two hundred and fifty thousand and anticipate living unto death on that windfall. Many (not all, of course) aren't interested in paying taxes to support infrastructures like schools and highways. They've bought their way into paradise and want to be left alone to enjoy it. Institutionalized selfishness is the keystone in an increasingly dysfunctional winner-take-all economic system that's traditionally been shared by poor and rich alike in America. But enduring societies tend to work off ideas about economic and cultural fairness. Such considerations are going to be increasingly important as the Latino and Asiatic populations grow and bring their complex list of demands to the culture.

A joke in Montana: "Nine months of winter, three months of company." Increasingly, from Taos to Glacier Park, the West is overrun with tourists: millions hiking and shopping for gaudy junk in the towns adjacent to the national parks. Locals love to complain, talking of tourists as a plague resembling locusts. But tourists can be managed. In Italy and Greece they're treated like a weed species that flowers money, which is not unlike the way they're seen in much of the outback. Westerners are learning.

Meanwhile, on the short-grass plains from the Dakotas to Texas, people are vacating, leaving. Twenty some ghost towns were abandoned in western Kansas within the last thirty years. In the last five years, eighty-three out of ninety-three counties in Nebraska have lost population, as did about half the counties in Montana and Wyoming. Towns where the median age is over seventy, and the main source of cash is social-security checks, are not unusual. This trend will accelerate as grazing, farming, and timbering lands, and lands with petroleum underneath and/or the possibility of open-pit coal mines, fall under the control of international corporations. The last best mountain-home sites, with trout in the pond down through the aspen, go to the very, very well-to-do. Many fear that the West is de-evolving—into gated centers of power and flyover zones between, agribusiness fields and clear-cutting, energy-extraction sacrifice areas and bombing ranges.

Meanwhile, thousands of poor people from Mexico and Central America risk their lives at the border to share a chance at realizing dreams of affluence and freedom. Who can blame them? All of us but the Indians were newcomers. But westerners have always regarded migrants, particularly those who want decent jobs, as invaders. During the Depression, itinerants to my part of eastern Oregon were despised as "Okies and Arkies." We see the poverty of others as a threat to our prerogatives and learn to look away. But cultures fail when our innate human sympathies harden into selfishness. That's one of history's enduring lessons.

Westerners like to think their society is based on egalitarian independence. "Take care of your own damned self." That's nonsense. The West isn't remotely capable of generating an independent economy. Since at least the era of transcontinental-railway building before the Civil War, towns and agriculture and lumbering and mining and petroleum drilling in the West have been nationally subsidized. The West is and has been dependent on a nation-and-worldwide system of economic interdependence. There is nothing wrong with that system. The original model was the family.

Established westerners, however, like to imagine that their hegemonies and privileges were independently earned, and are thus—because of some not too specific transaction involving generations of living locally—written in stone and untouchable. "My people settled this country. It's our country. The federals can stay home or watch their asses if they get in our road." Citizens given to making such claims seem to have forgotten that property rights are a privilege granted by a society. They build fences and lock gates, as they have since they moved in. Get crossways with them, and someone is apt to shoot holes in your mailbox with a deer rifle.

Many westerners feel protected by distance, like escapees after a jail break. At the Lakeview rodeos our sense of security was to some degree anchored on the notion that we were far from "the great world."

"Lock the gates," old-timers say. Newcomers, whether seeking the glories of sunrise alongside tarns above the tree line or a chance of finding petroleum reserves, tend to agree. "Lock it up after me." Native Americans smile. They know many of those gates are going to take a lot of locking.

☙

In *Dakota,* Kathleen Norris wrote that the idea of change, to many westerners, represents the threatening possibility of failure in the quite rigid social and economic systems they've used to ensure survival for generations. But changes are inevitable. In 1963, we had a single channel of television in the valley where I lived (the Beatles on the *Ed Sullivan Show* were like news from the moon). While I was probably the only local grieving over the fact that we were four or five hours from a well-stocked bookstore, our ideas of what to expect from the world were quickly shifting.

The first evidence, which I didn't understand at the time, was the passing of a generation of working men. I hired and fired (simultaneously cared for and exploited) field hands for our ranch, men who had survived the Depression because they were willing to do scrupulous work—combine men and diesel mechanics. But they were growing old and dying in bunkhouses. By the mid-1960s I couldn't hire men who cared much about their work. The young men from town knew that ranch work was a way to miss all the boats. Those who took our jobs despised both the work and themselves for being down to this. Pride in their capabilities, at the heart of traditional self-respect in America, was eroding. Now, of course, those workmen are being replaced by Mexicans and Asians and Central Americans.

But not all was lost. By 1972, when the 448-page *Whole Earth Catalog* won the National Book Award, a new version of the American countryside story was being worked out by young intellectuals and hippies, mostly urban kids from the middle class. It was a story founded on social fairness and on living local and grounded. In rural America, this involved caretaking and the use of proper tools—like using teams of workhorses instead of D9 Caterpillar tractors that tend to crush the ecosystem while harvesting timber. After all, why not care for nature if you can? It's what we have and all there's likely to be.

Popularized by intellectuals like Gary Snyder, Wallace

Stegner, and Ed Abbey, this ethos has been widely accepted over decades and is now a political force in the West. Traditionalists of the rigid kind who are unwilling to consider changes that impinge on their prerogatives are dying off. They're being replaced by well-educated activists who work hard at persuading their neighborhood and regional cultures, urban or rural, to evolve.

Not long ago I attended a Buddhist wedding with the peaks of Wyoming's Wind River Mountains looming off to the east in the autumn afternoon. Prayer flags swayed in a breeze. "Tiny winds behind great changes," a woman said, smiling but not entirely ironic.

Not far away, along the Green River in the summer of 1825, the isolated and individualistic nineteenth-century fur trappers would rendezvous on meadows. A decade later Narcissa Whitman and Eliza Spalding showed up on those same meadows, missionaries traveling west with their husbands, the first white women to cross the Rockies. Already, looming like the mountains, complicating and civilizing changes had arrived.

The evening before the wedding, at a nearby dude ranch, old friendships were renewed and new ones tickled into being during feasting and music. Guests ranged from mountaineers and herders and writers to the postmistress of the nearby town of Cora (she'd introduced the couple being married). Her rancher husband played his guitar, and her daughter led the singing. Ceramicists from Taos and photographers from Santa Barbara, hunting guides and cowhands and jewelers, country and city mice, wailed along.

I don't want to paint this scene too sweetly. The surrounding countryside was being seriously torn up and probed for petroleum deposits, and the local meth problem was said to be out of hand. Serious contention over grazing rights on public lands could have erupted. But folks got along that evening—most of them willing to take a run at new affiliations in a new West.

The wedding, elegantly conducted the next afternoon by a priest from the Zen Center in San Francisco, took place on a willow-lined and magpie-guarded sage-surrounded meadow. "Say what you want," a young man said. "We have to give back what we get. It's the road home."

A growing number of citizens in the West are eager to work out ideas they can believe in; they're dedicated to persuading their society to value economic fairness while preserving the natural world. Traveling the distances back in eastern Oregon, I'm asked if anything has changed since I left in 1967. "Sure," I say. "The world is rolling over."

Stockbrokers move west in order to work out of backland towns in Wyoming (trading on the exchanges in the morning and fishing the trout waters after eastern markets close at 2 p.m. their time). Oil-field roughnecks buy and sell secondhand Mercedes on eBay. Ranchers read the *New York Times* on the Internet and mull their responsibilities in showdowns like the one between farmers in the Klamath Basin of Oregon and the commercial fishermen where the Klamath River flows into the Pacific. The farmers need water for their crops, but without adequate stream flow salmon are dying in traditional waters. There's no solution that seems anywhere near win-win but informed citizens are rethinking options.

Many westerners are not only better informed, but increasingly experienced with the complex moral layering that casts lights and shadows across their encounters with a range of the multicultural travelers—Russian industrialists, Missouri cheerleaders, Turkish rug dealers—make your own list. Hard-handed men and women summer on Alaskan fishing boats, then head south to surf out the winter in the Mediterranean climate of western Australia. A friend told of almost drowning as he guided tourists on ocean-going rafts, taking them to stand on Antarctic ice. Talk moved to kayaking in southern Chile and salvaging aged barn-wood from Montana homesteads to be used as décor in Los Angeles and Las Vegas law offices. Making his living worldwide, my friend said, helped him deal with ironies. He was proud of the patience and flexibility he had learned to practice while making things work "out in the world."

Such experience is increasingly an element in the education of tough-minded do-gooders in the West. It's part of what they share, their own culture. At least ideologically descended from folk who cooked up the style detailed in the *Whole Earth Catalog,* they tend to shop in the same organic food stores, dress alike, read the same books, ride bicycles, and revere the same independent films and bluegrass musicians, and surely drink in the same taverns (a lot of tequila, it seems to me).

At the Lakeview rodeo, relationships were at bottom based on economics. We thought that property was sacred and reflected personal worth. This generation of do-gooders comes from all over the intellectual spectrum, but most of them would reject that notion. Their prime connection seems centered around the feeling that we all inhabit a commons—we have common laws and the Grand Canyon and freedom of speech and sandhill cranes congregating near the Platte River. We don't want to proceed without these items. They seem necessary in our society. There is a widespread belief that these essentials must be protected by our culture as a whole.

These new activists often band together in NGOs, nongovernmental organizations that are not necessarily based on political affiliations. NGOs are most often cause-based and range in size and influence from those with rich national and international memberships—the Trust for Public Land and the Nature Conservancy—to the very local, where citizens are dedicated to causes like preserving tiny endangered fish in hidden springs across the Sonoran desert or to economic justice for Latinos in the Colorado highlands. NGOs generate energetic volunteers and first-rate pro bono legal help; they're often well funded and articulate within the traditional political system.

Transitions in western thinking are likely to revolve around ways the people who presently populate western NGOs react to the mix of social and environmental questions that surround us. What do their members specifically want? How will they pursue their purposes?

Questions: How to visualize and create a "new" economy that responds to present-day realities rather than those of the past? How to simultaneously serve city neighborhoods and remnant rural communities as well as retirees, the aging, and even the hideaway wealthy? Can the West reconfigure its resource-extractive economy—agriculture, hard-rock mining, drilling for petroleum, and logging? How to answer a nation's demand for energy while preventing the petroleum- and coal-extraction industries from ruining natural systems like the Arctic Wildlife Refuge? Can we mitigate the oncoming evident disaster that is global warming?

The world is going through a crisis in matters of economic fairness. Can we provide for those left behind—poor whites and Native Americans on reservations and Latinos immigrating from the south and others from around the world? There are children searching Mexican dumps for food. Can we share our wealth with not only our own poor but the world's? Can we care for human communities and the systems of soil and climate and chemistries and invisibly tiny creatures upon which they depend?

Such questions, of course, don't count for much if the

idea of a rapidly oncoming end-of-the-world "rapture" and Second Coming makes sense. In 1981, the Secretary of Interior, James Watt, said, "God gave us these things [natural resources] to use. After the last tree is felled, Christ will come back." So, the question goes, "Why not ruin the world if it's going to disappear anyway?" It's hard to know how many westerners might agree with Secretary Watt, but let's hope it's not too many.

The West where I grew up was inflexible and because of that, irresponsible. At the Lakeview rodeo, my family never intended to sleep in the same hotel with the fellow my father knocked down the stairs—and they weren't going to roll out a bed in the brush between the bordellos. They were intent on preserving their status and privileges.

Citizens who base ethical judgments on rigid political, economic, or religious doctrines, however commonly accepted or deplored those notions may be, are at least partly dysfunctional in democratic societies because they have essentially abandoned their responsibility to work out problems for themselves. We hope future liberals and conservatives aren't blinded by concepts and precepts and don't turn into just another set of rigid, dogmatic "true believers." The quandaries westerners face will have to be flexibly resolved by the raggedy and the rich, up-country and downtown. Love life; maintain patience and strength of will while attempting generosity.

WILLIAM KITTREDGE grew up on a cattle ranch in southeastern Oregon and farmed there until he was thirty-three. After studying at the University of Iowa, he taught Creative Writing at the University of Montana for twenty-nine years and retired as Regents Professor of English and Creative Writing. Kittredge has held a Stegner Fellowship at Stanford and has received two writing fellowships from the National Endowment for the Arts, and two Pacific Northwest Bookseller's Awards for Excellence. He was the winner of the Montana Governor's Award for the Arts, co-winner of the Montanan Committee for the Humanities Award for Humanist of the Year, and winner of the PEN West Award for nonfiction book of the year. In 2006 he won the Chiles Award for service to Great Basin Culture, and in 2007 he won the Robert Kirsch Lifetime Achievement Award from the *Los Angeles Times*. He now lives in Missoula, Montana.

The Next Rodeo is set in Adobe Caslon, a typeface designed by Carol Twombly and based on the type designs of William Caslon, circa 1725. Caslon's work was influenced by the Dutch types of the late seventeenth century. Book design by Wendy Holdman, composed by Prism Publishing Center, and manufactured by Versa Press on acid-free paper.